San Diego Christian **College**
2100 Greenfield Drive
El Cajon, CA 92019

D0192441

PRAISE FOR
PATHWAYS OF DELIGHT

Dick Eastman shows biblically how the pathways
of extravagant worship practiced by King David are now
being restored globally in our generation through the
Harp and Bowl movement that combines worship and
intercessory prayer. There has never been a more exciting
time to be alive, nor a more exciting time to be a
part of the fulfillment of the worldwide harvest Jesus
commissioned in Matthew 28:19-20.

MIKE BICKLE
DIRECTOR, INTERNATIONAL HOUSE OF PRAYER OF KANSAS CITY

This work is not only a thorough, insightful
explanation of a fascinating subject, but it is also a
description of a radical biblical practice being reborn
in our day—something long prophesied but
never before attained.

JOHN DAWSON
FOUNDER, INTERNATIONAL RECONCILIATION COALITION

New Testament students too often overlook the wisdom of the Old Testament models that mentor healthy spiritual life for us today. Dick Eastman directs us as contemporary believers along the pathway of one of the Old Testament's greatest life-pattern guides: the Tabernacle of David then and our worship now! This book will open rich vistas of understanding for many.

JACK W. HAYFORD
CHANCELLOR/PASTOR
THE KING'S SEMINARY
THE CHURCH ON THE WAY

Pathways of Delight is one of the most refreshing books I have read. Dick Eastman's writing style is honest and enjoyable, and will bring you into a deeper relationship with the Lord. The linking of worship and evangelism is one of the major keys to releasing a massive end-time harvest into the nations.

CINDY JACOBS
COFOUNDER, GENERALS OF INTERCESSION

Pathways of Delight takes us into the very heart of what it means to war and to worship. Dick Eastman explains how the specific worship pathways King David followed, when he set up the Ark of God's presence, are the same pathways that are central to God's plan to fulfill the Great Commission. David's songs were warfare-worship songs; but they were also harvest songs—inviting a release of God's glory upon all the nations, so they would know Him. This is an exciting time to be alive! Church, let's cooperate with God's plan—in the way we worship and in the way we intercede—to bring people to Himself from every tribe, tongue and nation.

DUTCH SHEETS
AUTHOR, *INTERCESSORY PRAYER*

One morning I sat down to simply glance through a stack of manuscripts authors and publishers had sent to me; I had no time to review them. Three hours later, still in my pajamas but also in tears, I finished Dick Eastman's book *Pathways of Delight*. I literally couldn't stop. I had stumbled into a God encounter. This book is a roadmap to worship! Read it.

TOMMY TENNEY
GODCHASERS.NETWORK
AUTHOR, *THE GOD CHASERS* AND *GOD'S DREAM TEAM*

PATHWAYS

of

DELIGHT

2643
E13p

PATHWAYS

of

DELIGHT

DICK EASTMAN

Regal

From Gospel Light
Ventura, California, U.S.A.

Published by Regal Books
From Gospel Light*
Ventura, California, U.S.A.
Printed in the U.S.A.

Regal Books is a ministry of Gospel Light, an evangelical
Christian publisher dedicated to serving the local church. We
believe God's vision for Gospel Light is to provide church leaders
with biblical, user-friendly materials that will help them evangelize,
disciple and minister to children, youth and families.

It is our prayer that this Regal book will help you discover
biblical truth for your own life and help you meet the needs
of others. May God richly bless you.

*For a free catalog of resources from Regal Books/Gospel Light,
please call your Christian supplier or contact us at* 1-800-4-GOSPEL
or www.regalbooks.com.

Rights for publishing this book in other languages are contracted by
Gospel Light Worldwide, the international nonprofit ministry of
Gospel Light. Gospel Light Worldwide also provides publishing and
technical assistance to international publishers dedicated to producing
Sunday School and Vacation Bible School curricula and books in
the languages of the world. For additional information, visit
www.gospellightworldwide.org; write to Gospel Light Worldwide,
P.O. Box 3875, Ventura, CA 93006; or send an
e-mail to info@gospellightworldwide.org.

All Scripture quotations, unless otherwise indicated, are taken from the *Holy Bible, New International Version®*. Copyright © 1973, 1978, 1984 by International Bible Society. Used by permission of Zondervan Publishing House. All rights reserved.

Other versions used are

AMP—Scripture taken from *THE AMPLIFIED BIBLE*, Old Testament copyright © 1965, 1987 by the Zondervan Corporation. The Amplified New Testament copyright © 1958, 1987 by The Lockman Foundation. Used by permission.

KJV—*King James Version*. Authorized King James Version.

NASB—Scripture taken from the *New American Standard Bible*, © 1960, 1962, 1963, 1968, 1971, 1972, 1973, 1975, 1977 by The Lockman Foundation. Used by permission.

NKJV—Scripture taken from the *New King James Version*. Copyright © 1979, 1980, 1982 by Thomas Nelson, Inc. Used by permission. All rights reserved.

NLT—Scripture quotations marked *(NLT)* are taken from the *Holy Bible*, New Living Translation, copyright © 1996. Used by permission of Tyndale House Publishers, Inc., Wheaton, Illinois 60189. All rights reserved.

TLB—Scripture quotations marked (*TLB*) are taken from *The Living Bible,* copyright © 1971. Used by permission of Tyndale House Publishers, Inc., Wheaton, IL 60189. All rights reserved.

CONTENTS

A SONG FOR A STRANGER

"Is this a joke?" I asked the Lord as I looked at my watch lying on the nightstand. It was past midnight. I was in a bed I had never slept in, at the home of a businessman I had met only a few hours earlier.

Now God was instructing me to do something in worship that seemed odd—if not bizarre—in the presence of this stranger I was visiting.

This is not a joke, came the strong impression in my heart—an impression that I have come to recognize over the years as the still small voice of God.

The voice continued, *I want you to do it right after breakfast, when you share Every Home for Christ's 10-year ministry plan with Bill.*

Bill Williams is unique—a delightful man in his 70s, never married, who has a radical, though quiet, passion for God.[1] I first met Bill through Ruth Mizell, a board member for our ministry and a former White House aide to the first President George Bush. Ruth's husband, the late Wilmer "Vinegar Bend" Mizell, a congressman and professional baseball player, had also been on our board. When Wilmer passed away, Ruth agreed to take his place.

ONE STREAM

It was during Ruth's first board meeting that she heard the plans and details for our international ministry site, The Jericho Center. Our ministry had felt compelled to build this facility to help host consultations between organizations seeking to establish strategic partner alliances between ministries, churches and other organizations, thus helping to fulfill the Great Commission. Jericho, of course, was where God's tribes, though known for their bickering, murmuring and arguing, had come together as one to obey God in a divinely given strategy that resulted in His supernatural intervention.

I shared with the board my conviction that God was about to do a new work in Christ's Body, bringing its many tributaries together as one stream, and that we needed to be a part of it. I was careful to explain that although there had been many attempts to do this very thing (some with modest results), nothing compared to what was needed had been done. This could only happen, I explained, with God's supernatural intervention. It had to be a Jericho-like victory—complete unity welcoming God's intervention.

As I stressed at that meeting, it takes a supernatural work just to get a few core leaders united to pray about meaningfully working together. Many are too busy doing their own thing, as if they could finish the task alone. The fact is that all, or at least many, of these ministry efforts, if strategically woven together as one, could accomplish the task—practically overnight.

> God was about to do a new work in Christ's Body, bringing its many tributaries together as one stream.

I anticipated the question, How would this center be different from other similar projects? and responded with what I felt was the key. The center and its vision, I suggested, needed to be built around 24-hour-a-day intercessory worship—a combination of both intercession and worship that would saturate every consultation and planning session with God's presence and power.

I reminded the board of God's promise in Psalms that He is "enthroned in the praises of Israel [His people]" (Ps. 22:3, *NKJV*), and that He needed to be "enthroned" in all that we seek to do to partner with others in fulfilling the Great Commission. All these plans needed to be God-saturated.

I also reminded the board of something that I mentioned in the first book of this trilogy, *Heights of Delight*: The literal Japanese translation of Psalm 22:3 says, "When God's people praise Him, He brings a big chair and sits there."[2] We need God to bring a big chair (i.e., His throne) into these planning meetings and sit there, I suggested. Continuous worship will help make this happen.

Providing a further foundation for the board to understand the need for both worship and intercession at The Jericho Center, I drew their attention to Revelation 5:8-9, a passage quoted often in relation to the Harp and Bowl theme of intercessory worship.

And when he had taken it, the four living creatures and the twenty-four elders fell down before the Lamb. Each one had a harp and they were holding golden bowls full of incense, which are the prayers of the saints. And they sang a new song: "You are worthy to take the scroll and to open its seals, because you were slain, and with your blood you purchased men for God from every tribe and language and people and nation."

I read the passage and highlighted the fact that these heavenly worshipers came before Jesus, the Lamb, holding harps and bowls. The harp symbolizes worship and the bowls represent intercession. A new song is then sung that unmistakably focuses on the harvest. The song includes these words, "You were slain, and with your blood you purchased men for God from every tribe and language and people and nation" (Rev. 5:9).

"That is what we are about—" I told the board, "and not just us but all of Christ's Body! History's greatest harvest is yet to be gathered in, and the Church is about to come together as never before, saturated in a Harp and Bowl, intercessory-worship atmosphere. Intercession, saturated in worship, will create a climate for the most productive evangelism advances in history."

Ruth Mizell took it all in and, as is typical for Ruth, began to think of all the acquaintances with whom she felt the need to share this vision.

"Have you ever heard of Bill Williams?" Ruth asked me during a board-meeting break.

I did not recall ever hearing his name and responded, "Not that I recall, Ruth."

"He has continuous worship music playing in his homes, both here in the States and in Jerusalem."

Ruth then explained that in addition to Bill's residences in America, he had two side by side right in the heart of Jerusalem, one of which was devoted specifically to worship.

"I really think you should share this vision with Bill," Ruth suggested. I told Ruth I would be more than happy to do so, and Ruth offered to contact Bill on my behalf.

A SLEEPLESS NIGHT

She called Bill Williams that weekend. Three weeks later I found myself struggling to fall asleep in Bill's guest room at his residence in Texas. But sleep was not to come that night, and I was wide awake as the sun rose over the warm gulf waters of Galveston.

I am not sure I can do this, I thought, reflecting on what I was certain God had told me to do in the middle of the night. *How did I get myself into this?* I wondered.

I had arrived the night before just in time for dinner with Bill. After dinner, I was able to share briefly some of the plans of Every Home for Christ, and our goal of seeing campaigns established to visit every home on Earth with the gospel by the end of the year 2010. I suggested to Bill that I would like to share more about this plan just after breakfast the next morning, including details about how The Jericho Center could help make all this happen. Bill agreed.

Then we retired for the night. As I lay in bed, I could hear the soft worship music playing in the background. Ruth had been right—it never stopped. *What a beautiful, restful atmosphere,* I thought as I tried to drift off to sleep. And that is when I heard God speak.

I have a special message I want you to give Bill, came the impression. *My message includes two passages of Scripture: Psalm 27 and Psalm 149. I want you to share them as a gift for Bill right after breakfast.*

This seemed like a relatively easy thing to do, not unlike other assignments I have felt the Lord impress upon me when visiting people. But as I lay there thinking about reading these two passages to my new friend, the Lord added something startling.

I don't want you to read these passages to Bill, came the impression. *I want you to sing them over him—in his presence. I want you to do it right after breakfast.*

That is when I thought, *Is this a joke?*—a question for which I knew the answer as quickly as I had thought the question.

Understandably, I did not sleep the rest of the night. You do not go into the home of someone that you have met only a few hours before and sing a song over him— one that you have never sung before. At least I had never done that or known anyone who had.

As Bill and I sat down for breakfast, my heart was racing with the thought of the assignment given in the night. After breakfast I suggested the possibility of our praying together and Bill graciously agreed. I was inwardly wrestling with just how to explain to Bill my impressions the night before. Finally the courage came and I told my new friend what had happened.

"Bill," I said somewhat haltingly, "I believe God spoke to me in the night with a message for you."

Bill, not one for words, nodded and said simply, "That's good!"

I added, "Actually, Bill, God gave me two messages for you. Both are passages from Psalms."

Bill smiled and commented, "That's even better."

The difficult part had arrived.

"Bill," I said with a brief pause, "I believe God has told me I'm not to read these passages to you, but I'm to sing them over you."

With an inquisitive look, Bill just said, "That would be interesting."

I offered a brief spoken prayer, inviting God's presence, which really was an attempt at stalling until a little more courage came for me to sing. It is not uncommon for me to sing alone to the Lord, making up songs as I go. It is something I do almost daily with the psalms. But to do it in front of a stranger was a stretch.

SUDDEN SINGING

Suddenly I was singing, verse by verse, through the first psalm assigned, Psalm 27. I sang of David's one desire, that which he sought so passionately: to dwell in God's presence all his days, beholding His beauty (see v. 4). Then I sang of David shouting for joy in radical worship at His tabernacle (see v. 6). I was, however, totally oblivious to the unusual significance of what I was singing over this gentle brother whom I had met only the night before.

Turning quickly to Psalm 149, I continued my song. Now I was singing about God's people dancing before Him, making music with tambourine and harp, speaking His praise as they hold double-edged swords to carry out God's plan for the nations (see vv. 1-6).

How I ended my song I do not recall. I was numb. I looked up and observed a rather interesting expression on Bill's face. Again, his words were few. With a slight smile he said, "That was different."

Before I could say a word and as I was inwardly wondering if Bill Williams thought he had an oddball on his hands, he spoke. It was one of those out-of-left-field questions that you are not prepared to answer, yet hope that, as you hear it, you can somehow come up with a response that conveys even a small sense of understanding—even though you aren't sure what they're talking about.

"Dick," Bill asked, "have you ever thought much about what the Bible says in Acts 15 about the restoration of the Tabernacle of David in the last days?"

Like most believers who read their Bibles through on a regular basis, from Genesis to Revelation in the course of the year (a habit of mine for many years), I know it is not unusual to read something repeatedly and still miss its significance. Such was the case regarding the passage Bill referred to—Acts 15:16-18. I just did not remember it, although the phrase "Tabernacle of David" was familiar to me.

I turned quickly to the passage to see exactly what Bill meant while he began his own brief explanation. He referred to the fact that the apostle James, at a council in Jerusalem, talked about a time in the future when David's Tabernacle, or tent as it is sometimes translated, would be restored, leading to a great Gentile harvest.

Still clutching my *New Living Translation* Bible from which I had just sung, I glanced down and read the passage even as Bill continued speaking:

> Afterward I will return, and I will restore the fallen kingdom [tent, *NIV*] of David. From the ruins I will rebuild it, and I will restore it, so that the rest of humanity might find the Lord, including the Gentiles—all those I have called to be mine. This is what the Lord says, he who made these things known long ago (Acts 15:16-18, *NLT*).

I was frankly surprised that I had not caught the significance of this passage before, especially the remarkable correlation between David's kingdom (i.e., tent, or tabernacle) being restored "so that the rest of humanity might find the Lord" (v. 17). That last phrase especially captivated my attention.

DAVID'S SPIRIT

Shortly I would understand that the Acts 15 quotation by James was originally spoken by the prophet Amos, who had declared centuries earlier, "'In that day I will restore David's fallen tent. I will repair its broken places, restore its ruins, and build it as it used to be, so that they may possess the remnant of Edom [the Gentiles] and all the nations that bear my name,' declares the LORD, who will do these things" (Amos 9:11-12).

The passage continues, "'The days are coming,' declares the LORD, 'when the reaper will be overtaken by the plowman and the planter by the one treading grapes. New wine will drip from the mountains and flow from all the hills'" (v. 13).

As I gazed at the Acts passage, wondering about its relationship to the great end-time harvest that I was certain was coming, Bill shared something of his own journey regarding Acts 15 and the Tabernacle of David.

"Twenty-five years ago," Bill explained, "a strange but deep longing came over me to ask God to place the spirit of David on me. I even asked my Episcopal priest at the time if it was wrong to pray this, but he thought it was a good request."

Bill continued, "At that time God told me I would somehow be a part of seeing David's Tabernacle restored just as it says in Acts 15."

Caught even more off guard, I stammered to comment when I felt God speak to my heart again, *I brought you here because Acts 15:16-18 is the key to the fulfillment of my plans for the nations. You, too, will be a part of the answer to the prayer Bill prayed 25 years ago.*

Within a few months of this experience, my wife, Dee, and I were able to travel to Jerusalem

> David's Tabernacle would be a global movement of passionate praise and powerful prayer that would raise up the canopy of God's glory over every nation and people group on Earth.

to spend time worshiping with Bill in the beautiful place that God had given to him as a part of fulfilling his burden of 25 years earlier.

While in Jerusalem, God significantly increased my understanding of the role of David's fallen tent and how its restoration is clearly already under way—not as a physical structure, but as a spiritual edifice. David's Tabernacle would be, I felt, a global movement of passionate praise and powerful prayer that would raise up the canopy of God's glory over every nation and people group on Earth.

While in Jerusalem, I had the opportunity to visit various sites that were important in the life of David. I began researching every aspect I could about David's lifestyle of worship—and especially the significance of the small tent he set up in Jerusalem where the Ark of the Covenant was placed (see 2 Sam. 6:12-23; 1 Chron. 15).

Clear patterns began to emerge that helped me to understand just what we might expect if this spirit of intercessory worship, which I believe saturated David's original tent, were restored globally. And these pathways of delight, which will be described shortly, will happen, not only on a small scale on some tiny hill in Jerusalem, but in every city, town, village, rural area, people group and nation on Earth. The very climate, I believe, will be one of total transformation. To understand all this, we need to take a closer look at David's Tabernacle itself.

A CLASS OF ONE

It is a fascinating phrase—one of the most quoted of any biblical character in the Old or New Testaments. Often it is used to challenge men at gatherings like Promise Keepers. Rare is the study of the foundations of biblical leadership that you do not hear it: *a man after God's own heart*. And what follower of Jesus, man or woman, does not desire to become that?

Biblically speaking, however, those who qualified for this distinction represent a class of one. Only of David, the shepherd king who danced before the Lord with all his might, do we read this description (see 1 Sam. 13:14; 2 Sam. 6:14; Acts 13:22).

What made David, David? A look at other Old Testament characters and the space allotted to them in the Scriptures helps us see how David stands out. Fourteen Old Testament chapters tell Abraham's story. Eleven describe the events of Jacob's life, and some 14 relate the story of his son Joseph. Only 10 chapters are needed to detail the life of Elijah and his protégé, Elisha.

Then there is David. At least 66 chapters tell his story! There are about 1,200 references to David in Scripture, including 59 in the New Testament alone.

Kevin J. Conner, who provides the above facts in his remarkably detailed book, *The Tabernacle of David*, adds this insight:

> If we think of a character that speaks of faith, we think of Abraham, the father of all who believe. If we think of a man of weakness, we speak of Moses. . . . If we look for a man of miracles, we think of Elijah, or Elisha. But when we look for the Bible character for praise and worship, we speak of King David. He is the man after God's heart. The psalms of David are primarily worship psalms.[1]

Conner adds this interesting insight:

> While other ceremonials and ritualisms of the Old Testament passed to the cross and are abolished there, expressions of worship pass to the cross and through the cross into the New Covenant. Through the cross they become purified. Worship and praise will never be abolished. Worship and praise are eternal.[2]

A GOD-SATURATED LIFE

There is, of course, the enigma surrounding David's life: How could a man with such deep personal failure forever be described as "a man after God's own heart?" Familiar to most Bible students, even those with a rudimentary Sunday School exposure, is David's adultery with Bathsheba and his conspiracy to murder Bathsheba's husband, Uriah, a commander in David's army (see 2 Sam. 11:1-17).

This same David would shortly agonize before God over the sickness of the child born of that adultery. But his fasting and prayer would be of no avail and the child would die (see 2 Sam. 12:15-19). Soon he would weep before his Lord and compose a song of agonizing contrition, pleading for a restoration of God's joy and a pure heart. Hear his song once again—no doubt sung with tears:

> Against you, you only, have I sinned and done what is evil in your sight. . . . Create in me a pure heart, O God, and renew a steadfast spirit within me. Do not cast me from your presence or take your Holy Spirit from me. Restore to me the joy of your salvation and grant me a willing spirit, to sustain me (Ps. 51:4,10-12).

This is David, and somehow David is different, in ways not always easy to understand. If there is a secret to David's life, a key that explains his description as a man after God's own heart, it clearly has something to do with his all-consuming passion for the Lord. Philip Yancey perhaps explains it best in his book *Reaching for the Invisible God*. Yancey questions:

> David's secret? The two scenes, one a buoyant high and the other a devastating low, hint at an answer. Whether cart-wheeling behind the ark or lying prostrate on the ground for six straight

nights in contrition, David's strongest instinct was to relate his life to God. In comparison, nothing else mattered at all. All his poetry makes it clear, he led a God-saturated life.[3]

A PICTURE OF PRAISE AND POWER

This is the man who pitched a tent in Zion and who put within it the Ark of the Covenant. This tent would come to be known as the Tabernacle of David—a picture of praise and power, providing pathways of delight for the end-time church. Read again that passage from Acts introduced in chapter 1:

> After this I will return and will rebuild the tabernacle of David, which has fallen down; I will rebuild its ruins, and I will set it up; so that the rest of mankind may seek the LORD, even all the Gentiles who are called by My name, says the LORD who does all these things (Acts 15:16-17, *NKJV*).

The subject of the pages that follow is the incredible prophetic significance of David's Tabernacle (or tent) being restored in the end times, and the clear patterns of

Davidic worship (which we describe as *intercessory worship*) that will be a part of this restoration.

Central to this study is the extraordinary harvest of humankind pictured in the Acts 15 promise "that the rest of mankind may seek the LORD, even all the Gentiles" (v. 17, *NKJV*). The *New Living Translation* renders the passage: "that the rest of humanity might *find* the Lord, including the Gentiles" (emphasis added).

Before exploring in depth this interesting biblical picture and the various patterns of worship related to it, some brief historical background regarding David's tent might prove helpful. Brief attention to a few details now will be significantly helpful later.

J. T. Horger, writing in *Fundamental Revelation in Dramatic Symbol*, explains that it was approximately 1490 B.C. when Moses erected a temporary Tabernacle, which served until he built God's prescribed Tabernacle the same year. It was built according to the pattern Jehovah had given Moses on Mount Sinai, where the Israelites were camping at the time.

This Tabernacle and the Ark of the Covenant within it were transported by the Israelites throughout their wilderness wanderings for 40 years, and it continued to serve as their worship center for the next 350 years in

Canaan. Then, for at least 20 years, the Ark was neglected and left in a Gibeonite city in the house of Obed-edom, who may have been a Philistine! Finally, David retrieved the Ark and placed it in a temporary tent on Mount Zion, in the southwestern corner of Jerusalem.

David's tent, of course, would have been entirely insignificant without the Ark of the Covenant inside it. Of all the furniture in Moses' Tabernacle, the Ark was the most important. It meant to ancient Old Testament Israel what Jesus means to His New Testament Church. Mentioned 180 times in Scripture, the Ark was the very throne of God on Earth. To Israel, the Ark represented God's presence, His glory among His people.

On the top of the Ark was the mercy seat, and just below were two cherubim whose spreading wings served as a covering for the Ark (see Heb. 9:1-5). According to the New Testament, Jesus is our mercy seat—His shed blood covers our sins (see Rom. 3:20-27; 1 John 2:1-2). The Ark represented the presence of God on the Earth. Jesus came as the exact representation of His being—the fullness of the Godhead in bodily form (see Col. 1:19-20; 2:9-10; Heb. 1:1-3).

So David was desperate to bring the Ark home. There even seems to be a sense of urgency in his setting up a mere tent for the Ark. We read, "They brought the ark of the LORD and set it in its place inside the tent that David had pitched for it" (2 Sam. 6:17). He did not want to wait until he could build some glorious edifice to house the Ark which God had long before told Israel was the specific and literal place where He would dwell (see Exod. 25:22).

In the Acts 15 passage cited earlier, and also in its Amos 9 source, the Greek and Hebrew words for "tabernacle" suggest a simple tent. The Hebrew word used in Amos 9:11 is *sookah*, meaning "a tent, tabernacle, pavilion, booth or cottage" or even "a hut made of entwined boughs."[4] The Greek word used in Acts 15:16 for tabernacle or tent is *skene*, meaning "a tent or cloth hut."[5]

The Hebrew word used in 2 Samuel 6:17 to describe David setting up his tent is a different word from Amos 9. Here the Hebrew word *ohel* is used, but it similarly has the meaning of a tent, tabernacle, dwelling place, home or covering. It generally describes a covering or dwelling used by nomadic people (see Gen. 4:20; 13:5).

A COMING COVERING

It is the definition of "covering" that holds interesting significance when considering the Acts 15:16-18 prophecy.

These verses picture a last-days event, when the Tabernacle of David will be restored so that "the rest of humanity might find the Lord" (v. 17, *NLT*). As we shall see shortly, I believe that this covering relates to David's Tabernacle and that it is most certainly a covering of intercessory worship. Bear with me as I build my case for this coming covering.

First of all, we know this tent (ohel) was not fancy because the Bible says simply that David "pitched a tent for it [the Ark] in Jerusalem" (2 Chron. 1:4). Of this same event, we read of an earlier time when "they brought the ark of God and set it inside the tent that David had pitched for it" (1 Chron. 16:1).

Of course, one does not pitch a building. This was, as the text says, a simple tent, even though the word used also can be translated "tabernacle." But as Mike Bickle reminds us, "A tabernacle is a portable shrine. The tabernacle of King David that was used to house the Ark of God (or Ark of the Covenant) was a small tent—only about 10 or 15 feet high and long."[6]

Of this word "ohel," Kevin J. Conner writes, "Ohel . . . is used of a covering, a dwelling place, a home, a tabernacle or tent for cattle, for man, for families or for God Himself. It has both secular and sacred uses as a dwelling place for either man or for God."[7]

Citing the significance of its use in reference to David's Tabernacle, Conner adds, "The very fact that the Ark of the Covenant, where the Lord dwelt between the cherubim (2 Sam. 6:2) was placed in the Tabernacle of David (2 Sam. 6:17) shows that the 'ohel of David' was God's House, God's dwelling place, God's home."[8]

Conner also reminds us that the real truth of both the Hebrew and Greek words used in the prophecy of Amos and repeated in Acts is the fact they are fulfilled, first and foremost, in Jesus Christ, the Messiah.

> The symbolism of David's Tabernacle is vital to God's plan for the ages.

According to Conner, "He [Christ] is God's tent. He is God's tabernacle. He is God's booth. He is God's habitation. . . . He is the fulfillment of the tabernacle that David pitched."[9] Citing John 1:14, Conner adds, "He [Christ] took upon himself a human tabernacle, and 'pitched His tent among us.'"[10]

The symbolism of David's Tabernacle is obviously vital to God's plan for the ages. Further, it is essential we see the significance of why Amos prophesies that it would be rebuilt, or restored, at some point in the future, which James reiterates at that critical council in Jerusalem, high-lighting its purpose—"so that the rest of humanity might find the Lord" (Acts 15:17, *NLT*).

But why did God say He would rebuild David's Tabernacle? Why not Moses' tabernacle or even the far more glorious Temple of Solomon? Tommy Tenney, writing in his book *God's Favorite House*, reflects:

> David's makeshift shelter barely qualifies as a tabernacle when it is compared to the tabernacle of Moses, and certainly when compared to Solomon's temple. It amounted to little more than a tarp stretched over some tent poles to shield the ark from the sun and the elements. Yet God said, "I am going to rebuild that one." Evidently, *what is impressive to God and what is impressive to man are two different things.*[11]

THE DAYS OF OLD

Two additional vital, historical observations are essential to our understanding of what it is about David's Tabernacle that is to be restored and why. First is the historical and biblical context for the apostle James's referring to the future restoration of David's fallen tent; second is the historical context of the Amos prophecy itself.

Specifically, what exactly did Amos mean when he prophesied that David's fallen tent would be built "as it used to be" (Amos 9:11), or "as in the days of old" (*NKJV*)?

Kevin J. Conner, to whom this author is grateful for his historic detail of both the Acts and Amos passages, poses an interesting series of questions about why James was prompted to cite the Amos prophecy. Conner asks, "Why did the apostle James quote this passage from the prophet Amos? It seems to have nothing to do with the immediate context, either before or after. It seems that James takes it right out of context altogether in his use and application of it."[12]

Conner further queries, "Then, what has the rebuilding of the tabernacle of David got to do with the gentiles coming into the gospel dispensation? What is the Tabernacle of David? Why not have the gentiles come into the tabernacle of Moses?"[13]

It is clear that the primary reason James cites the Amos prophecy is to quell the dissension surfacing at the Council of Jerusalem regarding the growing conversion of Gentiles and whether they should be circumcised (see Acts

15:1-3). It was about A.D. 50-51 when the events of Acts 15 occurred. The Early Church was obviously advancing, with whole cities and regions being impacted by the gospel (see Acts 13:44,49; 14:1,3,21).

About 18 years earlier (around A.D. 33), the Holy Spirit had been poured out upon Jewish believers on the Day of Pentecost (see Acts 2:1-4). Eight years later (about A.D. 41), the same outpouring occurred among Gentile believers at the house of Cornelius (see Acts 10:25-48).

Tensions began to arise over issues of Gentile conversions and which aspects of Jewish law still applied to them. As Kevin Conner reminds us, the Early Church was in a significant period of transition, growing out of the Old Covenant with its heavy restrictions, laws and ceremonials, which often tended toward spiritual bondage. Now they were coming into the New Covenant with liberty in Christ.

Conner writes, "It looked as if the whole church would be rent into factions, two churches—a Jewish church and a Gentile church, thus dividing the body of Christ."[14]

Of further importance is to understand that the Early Church only had the Old Testament as its basis for what was unfolding. This was their guide, or as Conner observes, "their only court of appeal." They had to "discover the New Testament in the Old Testament."[15] Thus James, clearly inspired by the Holy Spirit, refers back to the Amos prophecy to build a case for the future Gentile harvest.

A VITAL KEY

James's prompting of the Holy Spirit to cite the prophecy of Amos is critical. Although the apostle was no doubt grateful in his heart that God brought this passage to his mind, he probably did not realize its unusual future significance. He was merely trying to build a case for growing Gentile conversions.

James was most certainly familiar with the Amos prophecy, which reads, "In that day I will restore David's fallen tent. I will repair its broken places, restore its ruins, and build it as it used to be" (Amos 9:11).

Note especially the phrase "build it as it used to be," or as rendered in the *King James Version*, "as in the days of old." Again I borrow heavily from Kevin J. Conner, who reminds us that Amos gave this prophecy during the days of Uzziah, the king of Judah while Jeroboam II was king of Israel (see Amos 1:1). This was more than 750 years before the birth of Christ.

Although the prophecy involved several surrounding Gentile nations as well as the Southern Kingdom of the house of Judah, it primarily concerned the Northern Kingdom of the house of Israel.

As Conner conveys, the house of Israel was in a back-slidden condition, a culture of almost complete apostasy. For 200 years, each king in Israel had perpetuated the golden calf system of worship established under Jeroboam I (see 1 Kings 12:25-33). Shortly after Amos's prophecy, God declared through Isaiah that calf-worshiping Israel would be captured by Assyria within 65 years and dispersed among the nations (see Isa. 7:8; Hos. 1:4; Amos 9:8).

It is with this historical understanding that Amos prophesies, "I will restore David's fallen tent . . . repair its broken places . . . and build it as it used to be" (Amos 9:11).

Here is a key to understanding this whole prophecy—and a vital key at that! To quote Conner, "Undoubtedly, in the minds of that generation, they [the people of Amos's day] would understand this utterance to speak of a restoration or revival of true and proper worship as was established in the days of King David."[16]

A COLLAPSING TENT

The people of Amos's day had strayed far from the practice of Davidic worship. There was no doubt that the

Tabernacle of David, as far as worship was concerned, had crumbled. And they knew Amos was not speaking of God raising up, or pitching, another literal tent. He was speaking of something having to do with the purity and passion of the worship associated with David's tent. That is what God would someday restore.

Conner concludes, "When the prophet [Amos] speaks of the fact that the Lord will build the tabernacle *as in the days of old* he is speaking of a restoration, an awakening, a revival of true worship that David established in his times at the pinnacle of the nation's response to the Lord."[17]

Sadly, it did not take long following David's death for the tent pegs of his spiritual house to loosen. Sin would soon topple it altogether.

When did David's tent (as a symbol of worship) actually begin to fall? We catch a glimpse when we read these instructions of the Lord to Solomon,

> As for you, if you walk before me in integrity of heart and uprightness, as David your father did, and do all I command . . . I will establish your royal throne over Israel forever, as I promised David your father. . . . But if you or your sons turn away from me and do not observe the commands

and decrees I have given you . . . then I will cut off
Israel . . . and will reject this temple (1 Kings 9:4-7).

Unfortunately, Solomon's encouraging beginning (see
1 Kings 3:5-14) had a sad conclusion (see 1 Kings 11:1-13).
Already during Solomon's reign, the tent had begun its
collapse. We read:

> As Solomon grew old, his wives turned his heart
> after other gods, and his heart was not fully devot-
> ed to the LORD his God, as the heart of David his
> father had been. So Solomon did evil in the eyes of
> the LORD; he did not follow the LORD completely,
> as David his father had done. The LORD became
> angry with Solomon because his heart had turned
> away from the LORD. . . . So the LORD said to
> Solomon, "Since this is your attitude . . . I will
> most certainly tear the kingdom away from you"
> (1 Kings 11:4,6,9-11).

Such was the spiritual condition of God's people
and the beginning of the decline of Davidic worship for
many generations. But, according to Amos, all that was
to change, and change remarkably at some future point

in history. "In that day," God said through Amos, "I will restore David's fallen tent" (Amos 9:11). The question is, When is "that day"?

THAT DAY!

There is irrefutable biblical evidence that we are living in the time that Amos referred to as "that day." The evidence is irrefutable because of the Amos prophecy itself. To fully grasp this we must read the rest of what Amos foretold:

> "The days are coming," declares the LORD, "when the reaper will be overtaken by the plowman and the planter by the one treading grapes. New wine will drip from the mountains and flow from all the hills. I will bring back my exiled people Israel; they will rebuild the ruined cities and live in them. They will plant vineyards and drink their wine; they will make gardens and eat their fruit. I will plant Israel in their own land never again to be uprooted from the land I have given them," says the LORD your God (Amos 9:13-15).

The expression "The days are coming" here refers to the same biblical context that Amos talked about two verses earlier when he prophesied, "In that day" (v. 11).

Robert Stearns, teaching on this theme of David's Tabernacle ultimately being restored, comments on these three significant words, "God doesn't say *some day*. He doesn't say *one day*. He doesn't say *occasionally*. God says *in that day*. He pinpoints a specific day in human history and says 'in that day' He intends to do certain things."[18]

> We are living in the time that Amos referred to as "that day."

Of course, the certain things God intends to do involve all that we read of in the entire Amos prophecy. Thus, David's fallen tent (a covering of global intercessory worship) will be restored when (and only when) the exiled people of Israel are brought back from being scattered everywhere and planted forever in their own land.

Who could dispute the fact that May 14, 1948, is the clearest possibility (if not the only possibility) for the beginning of this ultimate fulfillment of the prophecy of Amos? This was the day it was announced publicly that a new nation of Israel (the fifty-ninth in the United Nations) was established.

Today, most of us see that special day in 1948 simply as a remarkable historical fact and easily miss the totality of the miracle. Robert Stearns explains, "If you were to talk to an anthropologist or historian who studies history, cultures and societies, you'd find that in thousands of years of recorded human history, there is one anthropological anomaly. There is one unprecedented thing that has happened throughout all of recorded human history. It is the regathering of Israel into her land."[19]

BELIEF IN THE UNBELIEVABLE

Think of how unbelievable this 1948 miracle would have seemed to historians just a century ago. I thought of this recently when I came across an English edition of a unique book titled *Science and Faith: A Letter to Intellectual Friends*, originally published a few years ago in Chinese.[20]

Written by Dr. Edward W. Li, a gifted Chinese scientist who had come to faith in Christ, *Science and Faith* was originally a lengthy and comprehensive letter explaining to his unbelieving intellectual friends in China how he had come to believe the Bible and accept Christ as his personal Savior.

At length, Li explained how accurate the Bible is, particularly its many prophecies. He especially highlighted Israel becoming a new nation. Of this fact, Li wrote:

> There is no other nation that can compare with the Jews in the tribulation and disasters they have suffered. Besides the distresses of war caused by Assyria, Babylon and the Roman Empire, the persecutions that they suffered at the hands of European nations were almost as relentless.[21]

Li points out how in 1881 the czar of Russia was assassinated and 1 million Jews were slain in retaliation. Later, during World War I, the then czar of Russia compelled the Jews to leave and anyone refusing was slain by machine gun or grenade. Then, of course, came the massacre of Jews by Hitler during World War II. Of the 9 million Jews under Hitler's influence, 6 million of them were killed.

Dr. Li provides this conclusion:

> Israel, as a nation that suffered tremendous calamities, was diminished in population, scat-

tered to many different countries, stripped of its own land and nation, yet was never assimilated or destroyed. It . . . survived as a peculiar tribe preserving its special national tradition. This is a marvel in all of human history. Commonly in history, once a nation was conquered by others, it would not last over five hundred years. Powerful countries in history such as Babylon, Egypt and Rome, could not escape this fate. So, why was this weak and small country of Judea an exception? Historians cannot give an explanation.[22]

Biblically, however, we do have an explanation. God had set aside a particular day to do it. And we have the extraordinary privilege to be living in "that day."

Having said all this, I want to emphasize the totality of the Amos prophecy that James later cites during the Council of Jerusalem. Central to it is the restoration of David's Tabernacle so that "the rest of humanity might find the Lord, including the Gentiles" (Acts 15:17, *NLT*).

This means that just as the prophecy of Israel's return from exile has been fulfilled, so will the part about David's Tabernacle being restored be fulfilled. Further, this restoration will involve an unprecedented harvest of souls being brought into the Kingdom.

And that is why I have shared such detail regarding the whole of this prophecy regarding David's fallen tent. Could it be that the last great ingathering of people finding Christ will be preceded by an extraordinary movement of intercessory worship in the very spirit of passionate Davidic worship?

Could it be that the ultimate restoration of the Tabernacle of David (see Acts 15:16-18) actually refers to a supernatural tent, or covering, of worship and intercession that will be raised up by the Church in our generation over every tribe, tongue, people and nation on Earth? (see Rev. 5:8-10; 7:9-12).

If so, what can we learn from worship in David's day that we might expect will mark this movement? And how will it bring in history's greatest harvest? For starters, at least 10 pathways appear as we revisit David's ancient Tabernacle.

PATHWAY ONE:
CONTINUOUS WORSHIP
A FLAME UNENDING

Of David's Tabernacle, Tommy Tenney writes: "Nothing separated mankind from God's blue flame in David's house. In fact, *the only thing encircling God's presence in David's tabernacle were the worshipers* who ministered to Him 24 hours a day, 7 days a week, 365 days a year"[1]—for about 30 years!

One of the most distinctive characteristics of the pattern of worship surrounding David's tent in Jerusalem was the fact it was continuous. We see this in the description of the Ark as it is initially being placed in David's tent: "So he left Asaph and his relatives there before the ark of the covenant of the LORD, to minister before the ark continually, as every day's work required" (1 Chron. 16:37, *NASB*).

Later we read, "He left Zadok the priest and his relatives before the tabernacle of the LORD in the high place which was at Gibeon, to offer burnt offerings to the LORD on the altar of burnt offering continually morning and evening, even according to all that is written in the law of the LORD, which He commanded Israel" (1 Chron. 16:39-40, *NASB*).

Here we discover that worship before the Ark in David's tent was continual. Although some translators render the Hebrew word here, *tamiyd*, as "regularly," the essence of its meaning is "constantly."

"Tamiyd" literally means "to stretch." As an adjective, the word means "constant." As an adverb it means "constantly" or "continually." *Vine's Expository Dictionary of Old Testament Words* says that tamiyd "signifies what is to be done regularly or continuously without interruption."[2]

According to *Vine's*, "tamiyd" is first used in Exodus 25:30 where we read, "And thou shalt set upon the table showbread before me always" (*KJV*; *NASB* reads "at all times"). The fact that the word can denote uninterrupted activity is seen in other Scriptures where it is used. Isaiah said, "My lord, I stand continually [tamiyd] upon the watchtower in the daytime, and I am set in my ward whole nights" (Isa. 21:8, *KJV*).

Interestingly, it is this same Hebrew word that we find translated as "always" when God's visible presence is described as appearing at the Tabernacle of Moses. We read, "So it was always: the cloud covered it by day, and the appearance of fire by night" (Num. 9:16, *NKJV*). "Always" here does not mean that the cloud only came in the morning at a particular time and departed, nor that the fire came and left at nightfall. Always (tamiyd) here means that while the cloud was there, it was there continually, as was the fire at night.

When God said of Jerusalem, "Your walls are continually [tamiyd] before Me" (Isa. 49:16, *NKJV*), He did not mean just once a day, such as once in the morning or perhaps once at night, but nonstop.

We see further possible substantiation of this thought of never-ending worship in 1 Chronicles 9, which looks ahead to David's worship in the Temple after the Babylonian captivity and shows the order David has established. We read, "The musicians, all prominent Levites, lived at the Temple. They were exempt from all other responsibilities there since they were on duty at all hours" (1 Chron. 9:33, *NLT*). *The New International Version* translates the expression "at all hours" as "day and night."

It would seem quite logical that if the musicians lived at the Temple and were on duty "at all hours," the worship was continuous. Indeed, these worshipers actually were exempted from all other responsibilities because this was their specific focus.

We also see this emphasized in Psalm 134, which declares, "Praise the LORD, all you servants of the LORD who minister by night in the house of the LORD" (v. 1). This suggestion of ministering by night would support the idea that constant worship was being sustained.

The *New Living Translation* renders Psalm 134:1, "Oh bless the LORD, all you servants of the LORD, you who serve as night watchmen in the house of the LORD." Unfortunately, our connotation of a night watchman is a person who sits around reading a newspaper late at night in some deserted office building—perhaps with a periodic walk-through of the facility to check if everything is secure.

We know this is not the case here because the next verse says, "Lift your hands in holiness, and bless the LORD" (Ps. 134:2, *NLT*). These clearly are "watchmen worshipers."

A NEVER-ENDING PURSUIT

This theme of continuous worship dots the landscape of David's journey of intimacy toward the heart of God. When we read David's various psalms, we see his constant passion for continuous worship. On one occasion he sang, "I will extol the LORD at all times; his praise will always be on my lips" (Ps. 34:1).

Earlier we read one of David's most powerful declarations of desire, "One thing I ask of the LORD, this is what I seek: that I may dwell in the house of the LORD all the days of my life, to gaze upon the beauty of the LORD and to seek him in his temple" (Ps. 27:4). Little wonder that God called David a man after His own

> Continuous worship dots the landscape of David's journey of intimacy toward the heart of God.

heart (see Acts 13:22). He wanted to sit all day long and just look at his Lord!

A. W. Tozer captured something of this Davidic desire when he wrote, "It does not seem to be very well recognized that God's highest desire is that every one of his believing children should so love and so adore him that we are constantly in his presence, in Spirit and in truth."[3]

This wise worshiper adds, "True worship of God must be a constant and consistent attitude or state of mind within the believer."[4] So it was with David. David's pursuit of God was never ending.

It is this David who sets up a tent, brings in God's Ark and institutes unending worship. Of David's determination Tommy Tenney writes,

> David did two things to make sure God's presence remained in Jerusalem. First, he prepared a place for God's presence by constructing a tabernacle without walls or a veil. Second, he did something special once the Levites arrived at the tabernacle and set the Ark of the Covenant in place. He created a "living" mercy seat of worship in the tabernacle so God would be

pleased to sit and remain in that humble sanctuary.[5]

Suggesting that continuous worship as in David's day creates an open heaven, Tenney continues, "In David's day, the Levitical worshipers surrounded the ark of the covenant with continuous worship and praise. They enjoyed the benefits of a continuously open heaven because somebody stood in the gate and held it open."[6]

Intercessory worshipers, I believe, are these gatekeepers who hold open the gates of heaven. It is interesting to note that many Bible scholars (e.g., Matthew Henry, Adam Clark, John Wesley and others) believe that Psalm 24 is a song David sang when the Ark came into his tent in Jerusalem. Here David sang,

> Lift up your heads, O you gates; be lifted up, you ancient doors, that the King of glory may come in. Who is this King of glory? The LORD strong and mighty, the LORD mighty in battle (Ps. 24:7-8).

David's was a call to worship, no doubt inviting other worshipers to help him lift up these gates through worship. Perhaps it was this very song that first began the continuous worship in his tent.

A CASE FOR CONTINUING

Continuous worship, with the added ingredient of intercession, is so vital in the context of transforming our world for Jesus because Satan's opposition is also continuous. In Revelation 12:10, we are told that our enemy accuses God's people "day and night." In other words, there is never a moment that our enemy is not involved, in some manner, in seeking to hinder God's people and His work.

Thus, since Satan's warfare activities are continuous, it would seem logical that we ought to counteract his attacks continuously—24 hours a day—and not just in the traditional form of a 24-hour prayer chain but even corporately, on site, with many worshipers of all streams in Christ's Body coming together.

Years ago when I was first called into ministry, the Lord used a passage of Scripture in Isaiah to particularly influence me regarding this matter of continuous prayer. It would lead my wife and me to begin a prayer center in Sacramento, California, for college-aged youths. These young adults continued in prayer day and night for five years—more than 43,000 continuous hours! Isaiah declared,

> For Zion's sake I will not keep silent, for Jerusalem's
> sake I will not remain quiet, till her righteousness

shines out like the dawn, her salvation like a blazing torch. The nations will see your righteousness, and all kings your glory; you will be called by a new name that the mouth of the LORD will bestow. I have posted watchmen on your walls, O Jerusalem; they will never be silent day or night. You who call on the LORD, give yourselves no rest, and give him no rest till he establishes Jerusalem and makes her the praise of the earth (Isa. 62:1-2,6-7).

Again, as in so many passages like this, we see worship and watching linked to God's glory touching the nations. Note particularly the phrases "The nations will see your righteousness, and all kings your glory" (v. 2) and "till he establishes Jerusalem and makes her the praise of the earth" (v. 7). The goal, according to this admonition, is to watch continuously: "never be silent day or night" and "give yourselves no rest" (v. 6). Such watching in worship (which we are describing here as *intercessory worship*) will no doubt help make possible an open heaven over the earth so that the nations might see as the text declares, "your [God's] righteousness, and all kings your glory" (v. 2).

David certainly saw this key when he brought God's Ark into his tent and commissioned continuous worship.

As Tommy Tenney observes,

> David entertained God's presence continually for
> 36 years! He discovered a key that we need to redis-
> cover in our day. He did more than return God's
> presence to Jerusalem. He did more than display
> God's glory in an open tent without walls or a veil
> of separation. Somehow he managed to entertain
> God's presence in his humble tent and keep an
> open heaven over all Israel for almost 36 years!
> David's generation benefited from his worship.[7]

What were the benefits of this open heaven?
Prosperity and blessing accompanied David's rule unlike
any king before or after. Joseph Garlington writes, "One of
the simple reasons David's kingdom was extended beyond
any other kingdom was: David encountered and reached
more boundaries in his rule than any other. This happened because the primary aspect of David's kingdom was
worship and praise."[8]

Something in David did not want the flame of worship to die out in his Tabernacle. Perhaps he remembered
the Levitical directive that the flame was to continue
burning always in the Tabernacle of Moses (see Lev. 6:13).

The result was the extraordinary extension of David's kingdom.

A TASTE OF THE TABERNACLE

Interestingly, something uniquely similar happened many centuries later in the 1700s with the amazing extension of the Moravian movement in one of the great missionary advances in Church history. It was the Moravians who, under Count Nikolaus von Zinzendorf, began a prayer watch before the Lord that continued for more than 100 years. It was, to a small degree, a foretaste of the ultimate restoration of David's Tabernacle that I believe is unfolding in our generation.

It began in late August of 1727, when revival broke out among several hundred people who lived in a place called Herrnhut in Saxony (modern Germany). Made up of persecuted Christians from Bohemia and Moravia, Herrnhut—meaning "watch of the Lord"—was founded in 1722 at the estate of the wealthy and devout Count Nikolaus von Zinzendorf.

For the first five years of its existence, Herrnhut hardly lived up to its name, being wracked by dissension and open hostility. In early 1727, Zinzendorf and several others agreed together to seek God fervently for revival. It came gloriously on May 12. The entire community was transformed. Later Zinzendorf would write, "The whole place represented truly a visible habitation of God among men."[9]

A hunger for God intensified in the weeks following, and on August 27 a decision was made to cultivate this attitude and atmosphere, so it might continue. That day 24 men and 24 women covenanted together to spend one hour each day, at different times, in scheduled prayer. This was no short-term commitment and they fixed no date for concluding.

Historian A. J. Lewis later wrote, "For over a hundred years the members of the Moravian Church all shared in the 'hourly intercession.' At home and abroad, on land and sea, this prayer watch ascended unceasingly to the Lord."[10]

Some 95 years after this unique watch commenced, a journal was published documenting the growth of the Moravian movement. Titled *The Memorial Days of the Renewed Church of the Brethren*, the journal cited an Old Testament typology as a basis for this continuing watch: "The sacred fire was never permitted to go out on the altar (Leviticus 6:13) so in a congregation which is the temple of the living God, wherever He has his altar and fire, the intercession of his saints should incessantly rise up to Him."[11]

FRUIT FROM THE FLAME

What is most amazing about this continuous prayer watch was the extraordinary fruit it produced. Most mission historians refer to William Carey, the eighteenth-century British missionary to India, as the father of modern missions. However, Carey himself, when proposing his first mission to India in 1792 before a Baptist mission board in Kettering, England, used the Moravians as his example of extraordinary missionary advance. The Moravians had already sent out 300 missionaries to all parts of the world.

At the Kettering meeting, Carey, trying to build his case for a new missionary thrust to the East Indies, actually tossed on the table before his fellow Baptists a copy of a small booklet titled *Periodical Accounts of Moravian Missions*. Boldly, he challenged those brothers, "See what these Moravians have done. Can not we follow their example, and in obedience to our heavenly Master, go out into the world and preach the gospel to the heathen?"[12]

One example of fruit from the flame of 100 years of unending Moravian intercessory worship came in 1738, just 11 years after the prayer watch began. A small Moravian group had formed in London and was meeting regularly when a young searching sinner attended one of their meetings.

Something deeply moving occurred that night as this young man came to understand what it was that he had so desperately been seeking. Years later he would define that experience as his personal conversion, testifying that in that meeting his "heart was strangely warmed." His name was John Wesley, and he went on to lead one of England's greatest-ever spiritual awakenings. This awakening ultimately swept well beyond Britain's borders and blessed the whole world.

As we will discover in looking more carefully at the additional pathways, or characteristics, of David's Tabernacle which are to follow, something of what the Moravians

> White-hot worship from every tribe, tongue, people and nation will, indeed, send an unending flow of prayer-filled incense to the throne of God.

began is about to be remarkably restored. I believe it will involve far more of the Church than in Moravian days, and it will help lift a continuing canopy of praise and intercession over every part of our planet.

The flame of white-hot worship from every tribe, tongue, people and nation will, indeed, send an unending flow of prayer-filled incense to the throne of God. And that will be just the beginning!

PATHWAY TWO:
SKILLFUL WORSHIP
IN PURSUIT OF EXCELLENCE

"We are what we repeatedly do," Aristotle wrote. The philosopher added, "Excellence, then, is not an act but a habit."[1]

Long before the Greek philosopher offered this observation, Israel's King David practiced this axiom in his approach to worship. Prior to setting up his tent in Jerusalem, and much more so after, David desired that the worship he offered before the Lord would achieve a clear degree of excellence. He made certain all the musicians involved were skilled and well trained.

Perhaps David linked his understanding of the various Hebrew words used to describe God's glory—*kabowd, hadar, howd*—to his desire for the very best in worship at his tent and later in the Temple (which his son Solomon would complete almost 40 years afterward).

"Kabowd," for example, literally refers to the "weight" of God's presence or the substance of all He is and has.[2] It is associated with God's excellence. "Hadar" could be variously translated "glory," "magnificence," "excellence," "beauty" or "majesty."[3] But when David spoke of God's glory being present as the Ark was put into his tent on Mount Zion (see 1 Chron. 16:1,27), he used the word "howd." "Howd" means "grandeur, majesty or excellency."[4] At least two other times in Psalms, where God's glory is referred to using the Hebrew word "howd," we see it linked to the excellency of His Name. Note these passages:

O LORD, our Lord, how excellent is Your name in all the earth, who have set Your glory above the heavens! (Ps. 8:1, *NKJV*).

Let them praise the name of the LORD: for his name alone is excellent; his glory is above the earth and heaven (Ps. 148:13, *KJV*).

Everything about or related to God is truly excellent. When God's glory (kabowd) filled the temple (see 2 Chron. 5:14), the suggestion is that the full weight of His excellency saturated His house.

Of course, God's excellence is His perfection, His absolute holiness. Our problem with the term "holiness" is the way that we equate it to a standard of conduct (which, to an extent, it certainly does involve), rather than to how the expression relates specifically to God.

God is not holy merely because He does not smoke, drink, dance, go to movies or wear lipstick. I mention these because in the earliest days of my upbringing, in a sometimes rigid evangelical "holiness" theology, all of these were considered unholy. In our thinking holiness meant not to do these things—plus a long list of other things.

THE PERSONIFICATION OF EXCELLENCE

In reference to God, however, holiness is all about His absolute perfection. It is excellence with a capital *E*. He is excellence personified. God is uniquely perfect. Unique means "unlike any other; different from all others; having no like or equal."[5]

True, snowflakes are unique (no two are exactly alike), and the same can be said of people. Yet snowflakes and people are still very much alike. Only God is uniquely unique. And it is His perfection, or excellence, that makes this so.

It is interesting that the glorious angelic beings, those cherubim and seraphim worshiping around the throne, choose but one aspect of God's nature and character to verbalize endlessly. It is not His mercy or His grace (both beautiful aspects of who He is). It is not His power, might or majesty; nor is it His faithfulness or truth.

Actually, it is all of these put together. It is all of God's attributes (and those missing from this brief list) that make up His perfection, or completion. The angels cry "Holy, holy, holy" (Rev. 4:8; Isa. 6:3). They are even declaring it now—as you read these words—and they were voicing it when David set up his tent. Think of that! It is an eternal declaration of God's excellence.

David clearly coveted God's glory and excellence. We see something of this desire manifested in his careful attention to make worship before God the very best it could be. Consider David's selection of worship leaders:

All these men were under the direction of their fathers as they made music at the house of the

LORD. Their responsibilities included the playing of cymbals, lyres, and harps at the house of God. Asaph, Jeduthun, and Heman reported directly to the king. They and their families were all trained in making music before the LORD, and each of them—288 in all—was an accomplished musician. The musicians were appointed to their particular term of service by means of sacred lots, without regard to whether they were young or old, teacher or student (1 Chron. 25:6-8, *NLT*).

Several things are highlighted in this passage that are essential to our understanding of worship offered at the Tabernacle of David and what this might mean for us as this atmosphere is restored, dramatically and globally, in the last days. There are eight interesting observations that particularly stand out regarding this specialized force of worshipers that surrounded David's tent.

1. Mentored

First, the worshipers were mentored. There is something significant in the expression "All these men were under the direction of their fathers as they made music at the house of the LORD" (v. 6).

Mentoring has become a buzzword in recent years and has been possibly overused, if not misused. It certainly means more than casual contact, such as a Big Brother who takes a fatherless child to a ball game or a movie once a month. True mentoring is more like close-in (or even "live-in") discipleship.

Something of the origin of the word "mentor" might help us understand its intended meaning. Mentor was actually a character in Homer's poetic classic *The Odyssey*. Mentor was the loyal friend and adviser to the king of Ithaca. Mentor became the teacher and guardian of the king's son, Telemachus, while Odysseus went on his 10-year odyssey. Mentor did not spend just a few hours a week with the king's son—he lived with him in Ithaca while the king was gone.

It is this kind of close-in mentoring that our text suggests. Note especially the phrase "under the direction of their fathers." To me this almost has the tone of constant, in-your-face mentoring.

We also see from the text that the fathers doing this mentoring lived what they taught. Thus, these emerging worshipers were taught worship by those who practiced what they preached. They were mentored into their ministry.

As David's Tabernacle is restored in these last days, we should not be surprised to see considerably more attention given to training and mentoring worship leaders. I see the greatest and most skillful of our present worship leaders setting aside blocks of time from their busy schedules to teach other potentially gifted worship leaders their so-called trade secrets. Expect some of today's greatest worship composers to spend whole days (or longer) pouring insight into just a handful of other potentially gifted worship leaders who might multiply these skills.

2. Respected

Second, the worshipers were respected. The worship leaders at David's tent (and in the subsequent Temple of Solomon) were highly regarded for their work. This was not some auxiliary function of Tabernacle activity. Consider this easy-to-overlook detail: "Asaph, Jeduthun, and Heman reported directly to the king" (v. 6).

In today's American culture this would be equivalent to a person serving in the president's Cabinet. The fact that they reported directly to the king suggests they may even have been key advisers, not merely loyal subjects who periodically gave the king a report of their activities.

If the spirit of David's Tabernacle is to be restored in remarkable ways as this present generation unfolds, we should expect an amplification of this reality from David's day. It is not just that we will also respect worship leaders in greater ways by affirming their significance, but we will also see them as key strategic advisers in all our planning. Worship must be made central to every new endeavor, not just a segment of time set aside regularly in a worship service.

3. Equipped

Third, the worshipers were equipped. Note the expression "their responsibilities included the playing of cymbals, lyres, and harps" (v. 6). Later it says they "were all trained" (v. 7).

This orchestral array of instruments involved some manner of equipping and training. It also included an investment in the worshipers themselves, both of time for their training and resources for their instruments. (All this suggests the priority given to worship, a theme we will look at much more closely in an entire chapter devoted to worship as an absolute priority.)

In considering this observation as it relates to a last-days restoration of David's Tabernacle, we can expect much more attention being given to equipping entire congregations to be more effective as intercessory worshipers.

This, of course, takes time—much time. I see the day coming when considerable time is given directly within usual worship-service settings to help believers develop intercessory worship. (I have watched worship practitioners like Mike Bickle do this and have wondered why it is not done more!)

When, for example, was the last time you were at a regularly scheduled church service when time was devoted to teaching worshipers how to sing their own songs spontaneously to the Lord, followed by time devoted to actually doing it?

For most believers this would be unheard of today, but do not be surprised to see occasions like this occur in the future. It will all be a part of equipping worshipers to worship more skillfully.

4. Supported

A fourth observation is noteworthy and relates directly to the previous observation—the worshipers were supported. This insight stands out in our text: "All these men were under the direction of their fathers as they made music at the house of the LORD. . . . They and their families were all trained in making music" (vv. 6-7).

Often it is easy in a casual reading of a biblical passage to overlook brief, yet key, statements. Here we see just such a phrase, "They and their families" (v. 7). The *New International Version* translates this verse, "Along with their relatives—all of them trained and skilled . . . numbered 288." Some might interpret this to mean that worship was a family activity, passed on from generation to generation. One thing is clear: Some means of support had to be provided by the king to sustain all these families, or clans. These musicians were not merely equipped through some level of training, provided with instruments and told to go play as they felt led; they were housed and fed by the King. David had an all-encompassing worship strategy. It was the only way he could assure both continuous as well as skilled worship.

Again we contemplate how this might impact the global Church of our generation if in spirit David's Tabernacle is restored as it used to be (see Amos 9:11). I see God deeply touching the hearts of successful businesspeople and others blessed with resources to help them recognize the strategic value of supporting such sustained intercessory worship.

Many such businesspeople already understand the missionary enterprise and the costs required to effectively sustain it. Sadly, however, some look at worship and intercession as purely auxiliary—even secondary. Expect this to change as the spirit of David's Tabernacle is restored throughout the world. We can further anticipate that as intercessory worship grows, the harvest will grow as well!

5. Focused

Fifth, we discover that these skilled worshipers were focused. Like several other aspects on this brief list, this thought deserves a much closer look later in our overview of pathways of Davidic worship. It is a thought highlighted by the phrase "music for the LORD" (v. 7). The focus was not on their gifts or their music—and it was certainly not on entertainment. Their focus was on the Lord.

As the spirit of David's Tabernacle is restored in the days ahead, I strongly suspect that worship times in many settings of varied traditions will move increasingly toward a God-centered focus as compared to those typical "bless me" hymns or celebratory-type choruses that concentrate so much attention on our blessings, rather than on the Lord Himself.

6. Appointed

Another interesting fact stands out in this brief passage: Worshipers were appointed. This is highlighted in another easy-to-overlook phrase in our text where we read, "The musicians were appointed to their particular term of service by means of sacred lots" (v. 8).

The fact these worshipers had a term of service may well suggest this was some kind of a mission, not unlike a missionary today who is appointed to a term of service. After a certain number of years, the missionary takes a furlough. This is generally necessary because the worker needs a break. Their calling demands such a focus of intensity that time is needed for them to be restored.

Perhaps the day is coming when musicians, singers and other worshipers will give periods of time, whether short-term or long-term, to simply minister to the Lord in worship. They will be missionaries of intercessory worship.

As Every Home for Christ develops The Jericho Center vision mentioned in chapter 1, we envision numbers of worship and intercession leaders and teams coming for varied seasons to participate in leading continuous intercessory worship. Some, we believe, will be appointed and sent out from their congregations, both here and overseas, to participate in raising up a global covering of intercessory worship.

Some of these worshipers also may be supported full-time in this, as was suggested earlier of the musicians associated with David's tent. (The final chapter of this book will look much more carefully at the strategic nature of intercessory worship and how I believe many worshipers may someday find themselves involved in just such a worship mission.)

7. Diverse

A seventh interesting observation is also found in our text: Worshipers were diverse. Note the statement "The musicians were appointed . . . without regard to whether they were young or old, teacher or student" (v. 8). Of particular interest is the expression "without regard."

Look also at these two combinations of phrases in the passage: "young or old" and "teacher or student." This clearly describes diversity. According to Webster, "diversity" means "difference or variety."[6]

Recently I was speaking with my wife's parents in the living area of our home and noticed a video of a Gaither concert playing. It was one of those occasions when Bill and Gloria Gaither invited the old-timer quartets and gospel artists to come and sing their favorite songs.

One of those who was singing on the video was the gifted Audrey Mieir, who went to be with the Lord not long after that appearance. She was leading her classic chorus "His Name Is Wonderful"—a chorus that most worshipers of my generation remember well:

His Name Is Wonderful,
His Name is Wonderful,
His Name is Wonderful,
Jesus, my Lord;
He is the mighty King,
Master of everything,
His name is Wonderful,
Jesus, my Lord.

He's the great Shepherd,
The Rock of all ages,
Almighty God is He;

Bow down before Him,
Love and adore Him;
His name is Wonderful,
Jesus, my Lord.[7]

Shortly thereafter, I left Mom and Dad and got in our car to run an errand. I turned on the CD player to listen to a new CD someone at our office had given me of a popular contemporary singing group called Sonic Flood. (Yes, that is their name! In my generation groups had names like the Blackwood Brothers, the Couriers and the Happy Goodwins!) I somehow hit the track on the CD where Sonic Flood sang a contemporary chorus titled "Open the Eyes of My Heart."

I am not sure what I was listening to on my car radio just before playing that CD, so I have no recollection as to why the volume of the radio was set so high. All I know is that it seemed like an eternity before I could reach for the volume button to adjust it downward when that first guitar blast shook my Jeep Cherokee. I was certain that the earwax problem that I had seen my doctor for a few weeks earlier was completely healed. The speakers blared out,

> Open the eyes of my heart, Lord,
> Open the eyes of my heart,
> I want to see You,
> I want to see You.[8]

But then something unique happened in those moments. Unexpectedly, the car was filled with something more than words and sounds. It was a strange, awesome recognition of God's presence. It is hard to write these words without tears. I felt the glory of God.

This moving chorus that I had sung so often, and even led in many of our prayer and worship seminars, was alive with new power and passion. In that moment I knew that those who were singing were worshipers.

This may seem to some a stretch, but I sensed something Davidic in Sonic Flood's music. That something, I feel, was diversity; and diversity can be good. It is good because it touches us all right where we are. And we ought to get used to it, because the diversity in worship around God's throne should be awesome.

> Imagine these sounds blending miraculously to form one unique universal sound to bring God incredible glory.

Imagine every tongue, tribe, people and nation bringing their songs and sounds as we worship around God's throne (see Rev. 7:9-10). Further imagine these sounds blending miraculously to form one unique universal sound to bring God incredible glory.

8. Skilled

The last of our several observations from 1 Chronicles 25:6-8 is really the subject of the entire chapter: Worshipers were skilled. We read of David's worship leaders, "Each of them—288 in all—was an accomplished musician" (v. 7).

Earlier we highlighted this phrase from the text: "They . . . were all trained in making music" (v. 7). We might even assume from this passage that various ones of these worshipers played numerous instruments. One thing is certain: they were "accomplished" (v. 7), or "skilled" (*NIV*), in making music before the Lord.

Excellence was clearly David's pursuit when it came to worship. We see this when he finally brings the Ark from Gibeon and places it in his tent. We recall how the first attempt ended in failure and the death of Uzzah (see 1 Chron. 13:9-10), a fact we will look at more closely shortly. But when they treated the Ark properly, they did it with incredible attention to detail.

Here I simply highlight David's commitment to excellence in worship. We see this in the king's choice to head the whole operation of bringing the Ark up to Jerusalem. David appoints Kenaniah, a Levite specifically chosen because of his musical abilities. Scripture says, "Kenaniah, the head Levite, was chosen as the choir leader because of his skill" (1 Chron. 15:22, *NLT*).

Excellence in worship was always on David's mind. In one of his many psalms we read, "Sing to him a new song; play skillfully, and shout for joy" (Ps. 33:3).

As this intercessory worship movement continues to grow throughout the world, lifting a covering of fervent prayer and passionate praise globally and continually adding excellence to its intensity, it should not surprise us to see very skilled musicians devote their talents entirely to intercessory worship.

Some strategists such as Mike Bickle even believe that God may have something to do with placing a desire on the hearts of so many youths to develop musical skills, including masses of teens among the unconverted. When revival does finally come and large numbers of these young people find Christ, a huge army of skilled worshipers will be ready to help restore David's fallen tent.[9]

Others are equally committed to see this army of skilled warriors rise up globally, something I am convinced will lead to history's greatest harvest of souls (a thought I will build upon substantially a little later).

CHAPTER FOUR

A GATHERING UNTO HIM

Recently, when Dee and I were in Washington, D.C., for America's National Day of Prayer, we caught still another glimpse of David's Tabernacle being restored. A friend asked if we had ever heard of a ministry called A Gathering Unto Him. I had not heard of the ministry and soon discovered that those who founded it deliberately avoided attention. Publicity was not on their minds.

Established about a year earlier by a couple we will call Mark and Hannah, A Gathering Unto Him existed solely for developing and sustaining excellence in worship before God through skilled musicians. For many months, God had provided a beautiful facility within a few hundred yards of the U.S. vice president's mansion in the heart of Washington, D.C., for worship. I was told this was the highest point of the D.C. area and thus worship was flowing from this unique high place of our nation's capital.

Our friend told us that Mark and Hannah had already begun three hours of worship on Sundays through Fridays from 6:00 to 9:00 nightly. Not only that, but numerous musicians had come from different parts of the world, committed to make worship their primary objective. They agreed that they would have no other outside interests but would instead give of themselves totally to help build David's Tabernacle right there in Washington, D.C.

At dinner with Mark and Hannah, Dee and I were unusually blessed by the intensity of this couple's commitment to see a worldwide movement of intercessory worship develop. They openly declared they wanted to see a global restoration of the spirit of David's Tabernacle. This fascinated me because they had no idea of God's dealing with me on this subject, nor did they know of my friend Bill's burden as described in chapter 1.

Especially interesting was the fact Mark and Hannah had set a goal of seeing 288 skilled musicians (as in David's day) raised up to lead a much larger team that would ultimately lift this canopy of Davidic worship over every nation on Earth. I realized when I heard about this vision that it was incredibly ambitious and that this couple would no doubt experience intense spiritual warfare to fully birth it, but I felt it was of God.

Dee and I had the privilege of being a part of one evening of their skilled worship. What most impressed me was the fact that everything fully focused on the Lord. Nothing was done in any way that sought to entertain others who were present. Further, Mark and Hannah strongly emphasized the need for excellence, not perfection, so as not to exclude any person who truly wanted to worship.

Interestingly, many of the worshipers had come from distant places throughout the world to use their skills exclusively to worship the Lord. One young man showed me the harp he had made himself. It included a small piece of wood said to have come from a harp used in Jerusalem many centuries ago. He was delighted to use this instrument solely to worship the Lord. Further, Mark and Hannah used their own resources to support these committed musicians full-time. No one had to spend time visiting supporters or sending out letters appealing for funds. This, too, was uniquely Davidic to me.

That ministry is still in its infancy and not without challenges. Yet, it paints a picture of just how uniquely God is calling His people to restore David's tent of intercessory worship throughout the world. It is a call to a worship excellence, and many are responding to that call.

PATHWAY THREE:
CREATIVE WORSHIP
WIRED FOR WORSHIP

"Music is the gift of God to man!" Evangeline Booth wrote. The Salvation Army leader added, "Music is the only art of Heaven given to earth and the only art of earth we take back to Heaven. But music like every gift is only given to us in the seed. It is for us to unfold, and cultivate, that its wondrous blossoms may bless our own path and bless all those who meet us upon it."[1]

David certainly understood this gift and carefully sought to cultivate it. Worship surrounding the Tabernacle of David was clearly creative. This fact surfaces in an interesting observation regarding the moving of the Ark of God from the house of Abinadab as recorded in 1 Chronicles 13. We read, "They transported the Ark of God from the house of Abinadab on a new cart, with Uzzah and Ahio guiding it . . . singing and playing all kinds of musical instruments" (1 Chron. 13:7-8, *NLT*).

The expression "all kinds of musical instruments" is not without significance. David and those who served with him in developing their worship must have had a desire to be creative. It appears that they understood the beauty of combining the sounds of a variety of instruments in order to give God even more glory through their music.

The very reference to all kinds of musical instruments suggests a uniquely creative diversity. Jack Hayford speaks of this creativity in his inspiring book *Worship His Majesty*. Hayford observes:

There is a full spectrum of purposes and practices of song in worship. The breadth of style, the endless melodic possibilities, the delicate nuances of choral dynamics, the brilliant luster of instrumental arrangement, the soul-stirring anthems of anointed choirs, the rumbling magnificence of giant organs—all seem clearly to be God-given means for our endless expansion and creativity in worship.[2]

Heaven's Sound

Creativity in music does, indeed, have endless possibilities. Strangely, more than a century ago a noted church leader suggested the probability that all of the music in the world "would be used up" because there were only a "finite number of notes." He seemed convinced that if we were not careful, somehow no new music would be possible.[3]

David clearly lacked this fear. In fact, sometime after initially setting up his tent of worship, the king significantly strengthens that worship in preparation for the coming Temple that his son, Solomon, would eventually build. The Bible says that David made elaborate plans regarding those who would serve the Temple building project—including a vast contingent of worshipers.

Consider this biblical observation: "Four thousand [Levites] will work as gatekeepers, and another four thousand will praise the LORD with the musical instruments I have made" (1 Chron. 23:5, NLT). It is the expression "with the musical instruments I have made" that amplifies this thought of creativity. For some reason, David felt that the existing instruments of his day were simply not enough to do justice to the worship God deserved. So he created new musical instruments.

Joseph Garlington, in his timely book *Worship: The Pattern of Things in Heaven*, highlights an interesting fact about the Hebrew word *asah* that is translated "made" in this passage. The first appearance of "asah" in the Bible is in Genesis 1:7, which reads, "God made [asah] the firmament" *(NKJV)*. "Asah" is variously translated throughout the Old Testament as "to create, to fashion, to do, to make." Garlington comments, "God was giving David new music that couldn't be produced by existing musical instruments and methods. The only solution for this sweet psalmist was to create new instruments and methods to match the new music in his soul."[4]

Garlington provides an even fuller explanation of this idea that is worth examining, in depth, especially as we consider the unique creativity associated with Davidic worship at the king's tent. Garlington explains:

Step back to the time about 5,000 years ago when music and musical instruments were fairly primitive. King David began to hear new songs during his times of praise and worship before the Ark of the Covenant. This consummate worshiper, musician, praiser, and psalmist also wrote, prophesied, preached, and publicly declared things to the congregation of the Lord. He did all of it out of the psalmic mode. This man of the future was hearing and seeing things in the heavenlies, for which there were not earthly counterparts during his lifetime. It was up to him to bring what he saw in the heavenlies in vision and revelation back down to the earthly plane. He must have asked himself, "How do I reproduce the sound that I heard in the heavens?"[5]

It may be speculation as to what sounds David may have heard or even if he heard such sounds in the first place. It is clear that he made instruments to make specific sounds. It is also clear that heaven is the source of music. We see it at the beginning of creation (see Job 38:4-7) and we will see it again—literally saturating all of creation—at the culmination of this present age (see Rev. 5:13).

CREATION'S SONG

Concerning the creation and the earth being established, the Lord asks an interesting question of Job: "On what were its footings set, or who laid its cornerston—while the morning stars sang together and all the angels shouted for joy?" (Job 38:6-7). The very universe seemed to come alive in song as God spoke creation into being. Indeed, the whole of creation seemed born of a song!

Then as we look toward the culmination of God's plan for this present age, we see something remarkable—virtually everything created in the universe sings. We discover this universal song coming immediately following that heavenly worship ensemble (the elders and living creatures) who are holding harps and bowls and worshiping with "thousands upon thousands" of angels (Rev. 5:11). Together they sing, "Worthy is the Lamb, who was slain, to receive power and wealth and wisdom and strength and honor and glory and praise!" (v. 12).

> Virtually everything created in the universe sings.

Next, the truly unique thing happens. The text says, "Then I heard every creature in heaven and on earth and under the earth and on the sea, and all that is in them, singing: 'To him who sits on the throne and to the Lamb be praise and honor and glory and power, for ever and ever'" (v. 13). What is amazing about this song is that every living creature sings it! Notice again the words, "I heard every creature in heaven and on earth and under the earth and on the sea, and all that is in them, singing" (v. 13)!

Taking this literally, we must conclude that even the fish will sing this intelligent song of praise because they are creatures under the sea. Imagine that! Butterflies, bats, buzzards and bullfrogs singing! Cats and cows, coyotes and crows harmonizing. Warthogs and weasels, wombats and worms worshiping. I will stop here, but you get the picture. Talk about diversity!

Other passages of Scripture likewise suggest the whole of creation entering into worship. The psalmist said, "Everything on earth will worship you; they will sing your praises, shouting your name in glorious songs" (Ps. 66:4, *NLT*). King David himself sang, "Praise him, O heaven and earth, the seas and all that move in them" (Ps. 69:34, *NLT*). Later in Psalms we read, "Let the heavens be glad, and let the earth rejoice! Let the sea and everything in it shout his praise!" (Ps. 96:11, *NLT*).

All of these passages validate the reality that God created all creation for the purpose of worship. I am convinced it is for this reason He places within the hearts of His children a longing to be creative in worship. Indeed, it seems all of humankind is wired for worship—it is our intended destiny.

MIND MELODIES

A visit to Sandra Trehub's lab in Toronto, Canada, just might convince you music is already on our minds, even at birth. According to a *Newsweek* article titled "Music on the Mind," if you did happen across Trehub's lab, your first impression would be that you had wandered into one of those obnoxious preschool "superbaby" classes. You would see babies six to nine months old, almost transfixed, sitting silently in their parents' laps as classical music pours from speakers.[6]

But according to the article's author, the University of Toronto psychologist is not attempting to teach these infants some kind of introductory music appreciation class, but she is "trying to shed light on whether the human brain comes preloaded with music software the way a laptop comes preloaded with Windows."[7]

When Dr. Trehub varies pitch, tempo or the melodic contour of the music, these babies, according to the psychologist, can detect any of the three. The researcher adds that the fact infants recognize that a melody whose pitch or tempo has changed is still the same melody, suggests they have at least a "rudimentary knowledge of music's components."[8]

Other research has determined that the temporal lobes of the brain (located just behind the ears) act as a sort of music center. When a neurosurgeon stimulates these areas with a probe, patients sometimes hear tunes so vividly that some have asked, "Why is there a phonograph in the operating room?" The *Newsweek* article concludes that "the brain seems to be a sponge for music and, like a sponge in water, is changed by it."[9]

There seems little doubt that we are wired to worship and are connected to that purpose from the moment Christ comes into our hearts. Still, it must be cultivated. Practice is a key to creativity. As I mentioned in the first book of this trilogy (*Heights of Delight*), Brother Lawrence, the well-known seventeenth-century monk, referred to his life of worship as a continual

> We are wired to worship and are connected to that purpose from the moment Christ comes into our hearts.

conversation with God. He said, "There is not in this life a thing more delightful than that of a continual conversation with God. Those only can comprehend it who practice and experience it."[10]

The same must be said of worship. We must practice and experience it. As a youth, my instrument of choice was the trumpet. I am sure those early months of painful practice tortured my parents and siblings. I started with 30 minutes a day. A year later it was an hour, and then two hours.

But what began as torture became a delight. It also enabled me while in college to travel with a trumpet trio during the summer months on behalf of the school's public relations department. Not only was it fun, but I also earned scholarships for the following semesters. Practice was what made the difference.

FUTURE SOUNDS AND SONGS

I believe creativity will begin to flow in our worship if we follow the advice of Brother Lawrence. We must "practice and experience it." When David's Tabernacle was being established, worship was creative. All kinds of instruments blended together and David even made some new ones (see 1 Chron. 13:8; 23:5).

Joseph Garlington wrote, "What happened at David's tabernacle in the years before Solomon built the temple wasn't just a new sacrifice. God was birthing a new sound and a new song in his psalmist."[11]

As David's Tabernacle is being restored globally in the last days, we should expect awesome creative worship to flood the nations. This, of course, can only happen through God's people.

When God was confirming in my heart the necessity of having both 24-hour worship and intercession at The Jericho Center, I had a unique picture come to mind while describing this vision to a group of young people. They were participating in an intensive month-long discipleship training program. I explained that I believed God was going to send many youth groups, in addition to church worship teams, to spend entire nights of worship when this facility was completed.

When I suggested that I felt God was about to raise up a mighty army of radical, passionate, youthful worshipers, the room exploded with applause and even cheers. I explained that I saw these worshipers coming from all over the world, bringing with them their unique styles and, in some cases, exotic instruments.

As I continued speaking, I sensed God's gentle whisper

in my heart. He was saying, *I will give to young people who come for worship new songs, even songs in the night. They will be songs as beautiful as any you have ever heard—and these songs will bring Me glory to the ends of the earth.*

Immediately I thought of Jack Hayford, who had shared with me one day how he had heard, as an 11-year-old boy, a well-known composer of that day, Phil Kerr. The soloist was honoring God with songs born out of his own personal worship. In that moment young Jack Hayford sent a desire heavenward, "Oh God, someday let me honor you throughout the world with a song like that."

Today, there have been many choruses and hymns born out of Jack Hayford's life, but most memorable is his anointed anthem "Majesty." To my amazement, while visiting a house church in a remote mountain area of southern China in 1985, the believers there were already singing "Majesty" in their unique dialect. I was told it was being sung all over China. Jack's youthful desire had been granted. Few modern anthems have traversed the globe as much as "Majesty."

As I spoke to those young people, I thought of Jack's prayer as an 11-year-old, and I saw in my heart an explosion of similar passionate creativity coming upon youthful worshipers as they help restore David's fallen tent.

Reflecting on all this some days later, I read the words of Isaiah, who once looked toward a future remnant of diverse worshipers and wrote,

> But all who are left will shout and sing for joy. Those in the west will praise the LORD's majesty. In eastern lands give glory to the LORD. In the coastlands of the sea, praise the name of the LORD, the God of Israel. Listen to them as they sing to the LORD from the ends of the earth. Hear them singing praises to the Righteous One! (Isa. 24:14-16, *NLT*).

David's Tabernacle is, indeed, being restored and new sounds and songs are coming. One can almost hear them in the distance.

PATHWAY FOUR:
JOYFUL WORSHIP
A FESTIVAL OF JOY

Saint Augustine, in his work *Patrologica Latina*, wrote, "In the house of God there is never-ending festival; the angel choir makes eternal holiday; the presence of God's face gives joy that never fails. And from that everlasting, perpetual festivity there sounds in the ears of the heart a strain, mysterious, melodious, sweet—provided the world does not drown it."[1]

David tapped into heaven's never-ending festival. He understood something of its perpetual festivity. There was no drowning of heaven's melody in David's day. He heard heaven's sounds, sensed heaven's joy and entered into it with total abandon.

It is impossible to read through the accounts describing worship related to the Tabernacle of David, and the Temple that followed, without noticing the repeated references to the joyfulness demonstrated in Davidic worship. Joy was central to their adoration.

When the Ark of the Lord was brought to Jerusalem to be placed in David's tent, this description is given: "So all Israel brought up the Ark of the LORD's covenant to Jerusalem with shouts of joy, the blowing of horns and trumpets, the crashing of cymbals, and loud playing on harps and lyres" (1 Chron. 15:28, *NLT*).

This was not merely a pleasant sense of joy that was made manifest on this occasion, but the Bible describes their worship as including shouts of joy. David, too, joined in. We see this when he was describing his enjoyment at going into the Temple just to worship the Lord. He declares, "Then my head will be exalted above the enemies who surround me; at his tabernacle will I sacrifice with shouts of joy; I will sing and make music to the LORD" (Ps. 27:6).

Interestingly, there is no record of blood sacrifices at David's Tabernacle following the time it is set up on Mount

Zion until the Temple of Solomon is built. Here David seems to be saying that his sacrifices consisted of shouts of joy. If he did bring blood sacrifices, he did so with joyful shouting.

Either way, David was far different from Israel's previous leaders, like Moses, in this regard. David was not a priest in the first place, and yet he carried out this priestly function. And he did it joyfully.

A CONTINUING FEAST

Even when David admonished other worshipers to praise the Lord, he repeatedly instructed them to do it with joy. He declared, "But let the godly rejoice. Let them be glad in God's presence. Let them be filled with joy" (Ps. 68:3, *NLT*). Interestingly, this is a direct command. David is saying: Get happy, and then worship!

Elsewhere David sang, "The LORD is my strength and my shield; my heart trusts in him, and I am helped. My heart leaps for joy and I will give thanks to him in song" (Ps. 28:7). Increasingly, we understand why David was a man after God's own heart. He was constantly gazing into the face of God that Augustine suggested "gives joy that never fails."

There is no doubt that it was David's joy that led him so deeply into this life of worship and created within him a desire for more of God. David's was a continuing feast— a feast of worship.

Describing David's bringing up the Ark of God to Jerusalem, Jack Hayford writes, "His objective was to bring the Ark to Jerusalem, for David valued the worship of God. He knew the priceless worth of God's presence which always attends those who worship Him, and he prepared a new place for the Ark of God to dwell."[2]

Hayford concludes, "Upon the Ark's arrival, David conducted a great feast—a magnanimous event which beautifully illustrates that wherever worship is renewed, people will always be both filled with joy and fed."[3]

For David, his joyful feasting was on the wonder and beauty of God's presence and all of God's creation. Everything around him seemed to fuel that joy. A. W. Tozer highlighted this thought when he wrote, "Go to the Psalms and you will find David literally dancing with ecstatic delight as he gazes out upon the wonders of God's world."[4]

David was not an animist. He did not worship creation. But his heart exploded with joy when he saw God's handiwork in creation (see Ps. 19:1-4.)

Mike Bickle, who has developed an extraordinary 24-hour intercessory worship model in Kansas City, describes David's worship in terms of a feast of joy. Bickle writes, "Feasting on the beauty realm of God was a primary desire of David—and one of the secrets of this quality of worship (Ps. 27:4)." Bickle adds, "In fact, David was the first man to bring into one context worship singers, musicians and intercessors. I believe that many of the intercessory psalms were written on-site in the Tabernacle of David."[5]

FUEL FOR OUR FURNACES

Joy, apart from the fact it makes one feel good, has a practical function in prayer. Joy helps energize our time in God's presence. This is especially vital to the ministry of intercession, particularly in settings where intercession is to be sustained for any prolonged period.

Mike Bickle suggests that the Revelation 5:8 Harp and Bowl pattern of worship-saturated intercession is crucial to the joy needed to sustain the growing prayer movement globally. Bickle observes:

> I believe the harp and bowl model of intercessory worship is key to the present worldwide prayer

movement because it creates the "joy in the house of prayer" about which Isaiah prophesied (see Isa. 56:7). Our intercessory prayer furnaces can burn longer and brighter when they are fueled by love songs to God. As music and praise from the beauty realm of God are joined with the prayers of the saints and offered at the throne of God, great spiritual benefits are released on earth.[6]

Augustine's suggestion of a never-ending festival in the house of God is precisely what we tap into through our intercessory worship. In fact, no act that we can engage in identifies us more with the activity of heaven than that of intercessory worship (i.e., intercession in a context of worship).

Two particular activities occur continuously in heaven. First is worship, which has continued endlessly since the cherubim and seraphim, who were created for that purpose, began saying, "Holy, holy, holy" (see Isa. 6:2-3; Rev. 4:8). Second is intercession, which has continued since Jesus was resurrected and ascended to the right hand of God (see Rom. 8:34; Heb. 7:25).

Heaven's joy, or what Scripture refers to as "the joy of the LORD" (Neh. 8:10), is clearly essential to effective intercession and, for that matter, to any measure of balanced, practical Christian living. We do know that Jesus is interested in our joy. He longs that this joy be complete.

In the context of sharing His analogy of the vine and the branches (see John 15:1-7), Jesus said, "I have told you this so that my joy may be in you and that your joy may be complete" (John 15:11).

This word "complete" comes from the Greek word *telios*, which elsewhere is translated as "perfect" or "mature" (see Eph. 4:13; Phil. 3:15; Col. 1:28). However we might define it, He longs to see our joy perfected. Jesus wants us to experience the maturity of His joy.

THE FORCE OF JOY

What I've written about so far concerns our joy. What about God's joy? What does the expression "the joy of the Lord" actually mean? We do know that during a great revival feast Nehemiah said, "The joy of the LORD is your strength" (Neh. 8:10). This is certainly one of the most frequently quoted phrases about joy from the Bible. And most often we highlight the result of our experiencing this joy, rather than what this joy actually is or what it means to the Lord.

Not that this result—strength—is unimportant. Strength resulting from the Lord's joy, of course, is clearly a desperate need for a well-balanced Christian walk and especially for our praying. I recall Bible teacher Jerry Savelle teaching on this at a gathering of 5,000 university students in Fort Worth, Texas, years ago. In his message "The Force of Joy," Savelle cautioned:

> If I don't have joy,
> I won't have strength.
> If I don't have strength,
> I'm going to be weak.
> If I become weak,
> I cannot resist.
> If I cannot resist,
> the devil won't flee.
> If the devil won't flee,
> I cannot win.[7]

But, again, this concerns the need for and result of what Nehemiah referred to as "the joy of the Lord." We still need a good explanation as to what "the joy of the Lord" actually is. First of all, think about this as God's joy, not ours. Our worship gives God joy, but what is it that makes Him most happy? What gives Him maximum joy?

The answer might be found in the truth that Jesus shared when He gave His parables of the lost sheep and the lost coin (see Luke 15:1-10). In both of these parables, our Lord talks about the rejoicing that takes place in heaven when just one person repents.

Jesus concludes the parable of the lost coin by describing the joy experienced by the woman who finds the coin. Christ quotes the excited woman and adds His application, "In the same way, I tell you, there is rejoicing in the presence of the angels of God over one sinner who repents" (Luke 15:10). Of the parable about the lost sheep Jesus said, "Joy shall be in heaven over one sinner that repenteth" (Luke 15:7, *KJV*).

THE HAPPINESS OF HEAVEN

It is clear from these parables told by Jesus that heaven's highest joy is a harvest joy. Bringing people to Jesus makes heaven happy. Could this be the essence of the joy of the Lord? What could give God greater joy than seeing a person's life transformed in His Son? That's why He sent His Son in the first place. And when just one sinner repents, all of heaven breaks into ecstatic worship.

Perhaps the reason there is so much joy in heaven when people are converted is that each time a person repents and receives Christ, there is one more addition to that eternal chorus of worshipers. The apostle Paul amplified this idea when he told the Corinthian believers, "And as God's grace brings more and more people to Christ, there will be great thanksgiving, and God will receive more and more glory" (2 Cor. 4:15, *NLT*). The harvest, indeed, makes heaven happy; and intercessory worship, I believe, creates a climate for that harvest to expand dramatically.

> Heaven's highest joy is a harvest joy. Bringing people to Jesus makes heaven happy.

Traveling six to eight times around the world annually, my wife and I see much that must delight God's heart, both in worship as well as in the exploding harvest. In this I see a clear linkage: joyful worshipers make happy harvesters!

And here again, youth are especially being impacted. In an interview with Russell Shubin, Dr. Roberta King, associate professor of communication and ethnomusicology at Fuller Seminary, remarked, "Young people are responsive to music to such a degree that it's becoming one of the main channels of communication. God is gifting them to do worship, worship that cannot leave you alone. It transforms you."[8]

Dr. King continued, "We know that worship is not music alone, but in the music part of worship, God can speak in a very real and deep way. It inspires us to go out."[9]

The professor concluded, "So it becomes worship-evangelism, worship-discipleship. I think that's the gift of this generation."[10]

All of this, I believe, is related to David's fallen tent being lifted as a canopy of worship over all the world, resulting in a harvest of souls beyond our comprehension. As cited earlier, the apostle James reminded us that David's Tabernacle (tent) would be restored "so that the rest of humanity might find the LORD, including the Gentiles" (Acts 15:17, *NLT*).

The scope is obviously sweeping! Every Home for Christ's goal of working with all of Christ's Body to reach every home on Earth with the gospel in the coming decade is but one part of this sweeping objective. More than a billion homes have been visited in EHC's 55-year history, but our hearts are anticipating an equal number being reached in less than 10 years. That would achieve the goal of touching every home in all the world. In 55 years we have seen 27 million followed-up decisions for Christ but anticipate as many as 75 million new decisions in the next 10 years. Seventy-five million new decisions for Christ in one decade would be a clear outcome of the intercessory worship and the resulting harvest referred to in this book.[11]

Along with this, imagine many other strategies—such as the *Jesus* film, various church-planting initiatives, apostolic ministry and church networks along with denominational efforts, humanitarian and mercy missions, mobilization movements such as Operation Mobilization and Youth with a Mission, and a host of others—all knit together in an atmosphere of joyful intercessory worship. Only then can we begin to understand the joy that heaven must be anticipating. Davidic worship will clearly be central to it all. And it will be joyful. Heaven will be going nuts!

PATHWAY FIVE:
EXTRAVAGANT WORSHIP
RADICAL WORSHIP

With 134 musicians, the Vienna Philharmonic Orchestra is the largest major symphony in the world. The next largest would be the Berlin Philharmonic with 112. The rest of the top 10 include: the Orchestre de Paris with 111, the Chicago Symphony Orchestra with 110, the New York Philharmonic with 109, the Cleveland Orchestra with 108, the London Royal Opera with 106, the Los Angeles Philharmonic with

105, the Philadelphia Orchestra with 104 and the Boston Symphony Orchestra with 98.

If you combined all these musicians into one vast symphony, there would be 1,097 participants. Then add to their number all the musicians of the 30 next largest orchestras in the world (each with at least 80 musicians), and you would have an extraordinary symphony consisting of more than 3,500 musicians.

You would, however, come up hundreds of musicians short of the 4,000 David employed for his Tabernacle worship (see 1 Chron. 23:5). David was an extravagant worshiper!

"Extravagant" means "exceeding the limits" or "excessively elaborate." It is derived from the Latin words *extra*, meaning "outside" or "beyond," and *vagari*, meaning "to wander." Thus, "to wander outside" becomes "exceeding the limits" or going out of bounds.[1] "Extravagant" is synonymous with "lavish," "unrestrained," "exorbitant" and "fantastic." Applied to the Tabernacle of David's day, extravagant worship meant radical worship.

One of the more interesting aspects about worship related to David's Tabernacle, and Davidic worship in general, concerns its extravagance. Perhaps, to some degree, all of the pathways, or facts, about the Tabernacle of David that we are examining are summed up in this one observation: Everything about the worship David inaugurated and sustained was extravagant. David was a lavish worshiper and he cultivated lavish worship.

A CELEBRATION OF EXTRAVAGANCE

Notice what the Bible says regarding the Ark of God in David's first attempt to move it back to Jerusalem: "David and all Israel were celebrating before God with all their might, singing and playing all kinds of musical instruments—lyres, harps, tambourines, cymbals, and trumpets" (1 Chron. 13:8, *NLT*).

True, the sad episode regarding the death of Uzzah occurs, and there were vital lessons for David to learn through this mistake, which we will examine later; but it is hard to overlook expressions in this passage like "celebrating . . . with all their might" and "playing all kinds of musical instruments" (v. 8, *NLT*).

This is not the only instance when Davidic worship is described in connection with such expressions of extravagance as "all their might" or "celebrating." Later we read the following description of moving the Ark: "Then David and the leaders of Israel and the generals of the army went to the home of Obed-edom to bring the Ark of the LORD's covenant up to Jerusalem with a great celebration" (1 Chron. 15:25, *NLT*).

When examining this extravagance in the context of Davidic worship, one can only imagine all that the expression "with a great celebration" really conveys. We do know that David not only encouraged such celebrating—he led the way.

When the Ark finally reaches Jerusalem, we read this familiar passage: "And David danced before the LORD with all his might, wearing a priestly tunic. So David and all Israel brought up the Ark of the LORD with much shouting and blowing trumpets" (2 Sam. 6:14-15, *NLT*). More extravagance! Here we see something said of a king in Israel that is never said of another. Nowhere else in the Old Testament do we read of a king dancing before the Lord with all his might. Little wonder God describes David as "a man after my own heart" (Acts 13:22). David led the way in extravagant worship. Davidic worship was a celebration of extravagance.

But perhaps one of the most interesting insights regarding the moving of the Ark of God into Jerusalem in David's day was the very extravagance that accompanied the move. We know that the Ark had been in Gibeon for some months because David was afraid to move it after the first and improper attempt had failed.

A FAILURE OF WORSHIP

For that first attempt David had a cart constructed to carry the Ark, no doubt to expedite the journey (see 2 Sam. 6:3-4). It appears he was anxious, perhaps desperate, to obtain the Ark from the house of Abinadab, and it just made sense to do it this way. Then, too, the Ark was probably unusually heavy, being overlaid with pure gold, including the two solid gold cherubim sitting atop. David no doubt knew the Philistines moved the Ark in this manner. So why couldn't he do the same?

It is clear David never sought God about this matter (see 1 Chron. 15:13), or God would have told him clearly it was being handled improperly. Elsewhere in David's life we see him directly asking God for guidance in such matters, and God very specifically answers (see 2 Sam. 5:17-20,22-25). But this time he did not bother to ask.

At the threshing floor of Nacon, God allows the oxen to stumble and the Ark suddenly shifts (see 2 Sam. 6:6). Because the Ark appears to be slipping and may crash to the ground, Uzzah reaches to steady it.

It is not a pleasant picture, and a phrase in the text is still troubling: "God struck him down and he died" (2 Sam. 6:7). The *New Living Translation* is more blunt:

"Then the LORD's anger blazed out against Uzzah for doing this, and God struck him dead."

If this troubles our theology, then imagine how David felt! He decided to leave the Ark at the home of Obed-edom and went back to Jerusalem discouraged. For three months he brooded, perhaps complained, and no doubt asked God why. He learned that God had long before given concise directions on how the Ark was to be moved—by using poles attached to the Ark, and these were only to be carried on the shoulders of sanctified Levites. If David knew all this and simply disobeyed, it is easier to understand God's displeasure. If such were the case, perhaps these several months before that final move were spent by David in careful reflection and repentance.

David's courage finally returns and he heads for the home of Obed-edom in Gibeon to bring the Ark back properly. And it is here that we see something potentially remarkable about David's extravagance in worship.

A SACRIFICE EVERY SIX STEPS

There's an easy-to-overlook statement in the text of this event at Gibeon that has unusual implications. We read, "After the men who were carrying it had gone six steps, they stopped and waited so David could sacrifice an ox and a fattened calf" (2 Sam. 6:13, *NLT*).

It is at least six miles from Gibeon to where the Ark was finally placed in Jerusalem (it may have been as much as a 10-mile journey).[2] For the purpose of illustration here, we will use the six-mile figure.

Some Bible teachers have suggested the possibility (though others might question the inference) that David did not stop just once after the first six steps to offer a sacrifice but that he was so afraid of not honoring God properly in this second attempt of moving the Ark that he may have stopped every six steps for the entire journey of at least six miles. This theory suggests that at every stop he would have offered similar sacrifices.[3]

A friend once suggested that some discoveries were possible, probable or provable.[4] My conclusion about the inference of this journey from Gibeon to Jerusalem is that it is at least possible that David's contingent paused every six paces, or steps, for the entire journey, simply because of David's tendency toward extravagance.

I arrive at this inference after examining everything else David did in worship. Nothing was cheap or second-rate. He may have slipped up with the cart and Uzzah, but when it came to worship, David went all out.

Knowing David, it is just hard to believe in light of the seriousness of the situation that he would offer only one ox and one fattened calf. Further, would not David have offered this simple sacrifice at the very start of the journey if it was to be a one-time act? Why would he take six steps and then do it? To me, this is not the David I have discovered in my studies of his passion and pursuit of God.

If the processional did stop every six steps, it adds even more interesting speculation to the potential extravagance of David's worship.

If we consider that each step is approximately 2 feet, 2 inches, we could conclude that six steps would be approximately 13 feet, give or take a foot or two for tall Levites! Stopping every six steps for six miles would have required an amazing 2,437 stops over the course of those six miles, breaking down to about 406 stops per mile. Here I have some sympathy for those who believe David stopped only once; it just seems too impossible to have stopped so often.

But what if this indeed did happen? Further, imagine the number of sacrifices made and the total time required to accomplish such a feat. It would require 2,437 oxen and an equal number of calves. Assuming it would take at least 30 minutes to perform each dual sacrifice, the total time required would be 1,218 hours, or 51 days!

We must also consider that however large the group that accompanied this processional may have been, it would certainly necessitate pauses to eat and sleep if indeed it occurred over so many days. If we allowed eight hours for sleep each night and three hours for daily meals, then 1,031 additional hours, or 43 additional days, would be required.

Amazingly, to accomplish all of these necessities for the move of the Ark six miles from Gibeon to Jerusalem would have required 94 days. I can understand those who consider this unlikely, but knowing David, it would not surprise me in the least. Whether or not David did stop every six steps to offer a worship sacrifice, the point is still made: David was an extravagant worshiper. All that David did in regard to worshiping God was extravagant.

A LIFE OF LAVISH GIVING

As David's life nears its end, we see this same extravagance. He has given his son Solomon detailed instructions regarding the building of a permanent Temple. David himself gives a lavish, clearly extravagant gift toward this task. His own testimony reads, "And now because of my devotion to the Temple of my God, I am giving all of my own private treasures of gold and silver to help in the construction" (1 Chron. 29:3, *NLT*).

The text goes on to say that 3,000 talents of gold were given, which amounts to approximately 112 tons. Additionally, some 262 tons of refined silver were a part of David's extravagant sacrifice (see v. 4, *NLT*).

The king then issued an invitation for those willing to participate. David declares, "Now then, who will follow my example? Who is willing to give offerings to the LORD today?" (v. 5, *NLT*). The results were astounding. Not only had David's worship been extravagant, but now everyone's worship in giving also becomes extravagant. It was lavish, even fantastic!

The *New Living Translation* tells us the total offering included some 188 tons of gold, 10,000 additional gold coins, 375 tons of silver, approximately 675 tons of bronze and about 3,750 tons of iron (see v. 7, *NLT*).

Could it be that as the spirit of David's Tabernacle (i.e., an extraordinary movement of intercessory worship) is restored globally in the last days, we will not only see lavish worship released but a resulting extravagance in giving? I saw just a glimpse of something like this when I first taught these pathways of Davidic worship at a Harp and Bowl intercessory worship conference in Hong Kong.

A WINDOW FOR WORSHIP

Dee and I had been invited to Hong Kong over the 2000 Easter season to help lead what would become an annual Harp and Bowl conference. I had been there a year earlier for a conference focusing intercession on the 10/40 Window—that geographic area of the world so designated by its longitudinal lines (10 degrees north and 40 degrees north) and stretching from West Africa to Japan and including the Middle East. (This phrase was coined by Luis Bush, a founder of the AD2000 and Beyond Movement. The 10/40 Window is home to 95 percent of the world's least-evangelized people groups and became a well-known prayer focus throughout the evangelical community in the 1990s.)

As we contemplated returning for a follow-up conference, those involved in the planning agreed it should carry the Harp and Bowl intercessory worship theme, which has now become an annual Hong Kong event. Just as the earlier theme had been Pray Through the Window, this emphasis would encourage Worship Through the Window.

That first Harp and Bowl conference, for both Dee and myself, was to become a highlight of our 37 years of marriage and ministry. From the onset of the planning, it was decided that we would set aside larger blocks of time to actually practice what we would be teaching. Mark Geppert, a radical worshiper who for years has led intercessory worship teams on prayer walks in Asia and elsewhere, agreed to help lead the five-day conference.

Because it was our intention to have prolonged seasons of worship, including focused intercession, a special worship team was developed to help sustain the worship. I knew it would be an experiment because we had never attempted something like this in a large multichurch setting. In fact, most participants would be from traditional mainline denominations in Hong Kong.

A SPIRIT OF EXTRAVAGANCE

As the conference began, I wondered how successful it was going to be. I deliberately taught very short sessions, from 20 to 30 minutes in length, including time for translation into Chinese. Then the worship team and I would lead the congregation into what I hoped would become seasons of intercessory worship.

However, as we went into our first worship segment, it seemed to be nothing more than a typical time of worship—not unlike many contemporary churches experience every Sunday morning.

Then something happened. At the conclusion of a particularly worshipful chorus, spontaneous singing began. As the musicians followed along, we heard the blending of a thousand voices, each singing his or her own song, creating an unusual atmosphere of worship that would recur throughout the conference and would build as each day progressed. These worshipers were also beginning to create what I now believe was a spirit of extravagant worship.

> We heard the blending of a thousand voices, each singing his or her own song, creating an unusual atmosphere of worship.

Because the Harp and Bowl symbolism of Revelation 5:8-10 focuses on a great harvest of souls coming from "every tribe and language and people and nation" (v. 9), the host of the conference, Dr. Agatha Chan, expressed her desire to see a special offering received for spreading the gospel throughout the nations, especially the 10/40 Window. Agatha asked me when I felt it might be appropriate to receive such an offering. I suggested perhaps it would be good to do it on the day I taught specifically about the Tabernacle of David being restored (see Acts 15:16-18), because this prophesy speaks of all the Gentiles (nations) being given the gospel. Little did I realize how significant that decision would be.

The day of the offering just happened to be Easter Sunday, the fourth day of the conference. I had intended to teach all 10 pathways of Davidic worship in two brief segments that afternoon. Because the entire session was to be three hours long, I thought I would share five aspects for about 30 minutes, then lead in an hour of intercessory worship and then do the same with the remaining five pathways.

Agatha and I agreed that we would take the offering sometime in the middle of the afternoon but decided to make it a part of the worship, rather than stop everything for an offering. After all, giving is clearly an act of worship. Passing offering plates seemed too formal and would, we felt, interrupt the worship, so the idea came to set cardboard boxes at the front of the auditorium and let people bring their gifts as an act of worship, if they so desired.

I initially thought this might hinder the offering because not everyone would respond, but both Agatha and I agreed it would be less disruptive because it would not involve stopping to have ushers pass offering plates.

WANDERING IN LAVISH WORSHIP

As I very briefly taught the fifth aspect of worship at David's Tabernacle—that it was extravagant—I mentioned that we would soon go into a sustained time of intercessory worship and that during that time, all those who wanted to give "willingly" (1 Chron. 29:6), just as in David's day, to specifically bless the nations, could bring their gift and place it in one of the boxes. But first, I told them, we wanted to devote considerable time to identify with the first aspect of Davidic worship that I had taught a few minutes earlier in that session—the fact that worship at David's tent was continuous.

I explained, of course, that we would not be doing this for 24 hours continuously but that we could imagine over the next hour or so joining with those exalted angelic beings around the throne who continuously praise God purely for His holiness (see Isa. 6:2-3; Rev. 4:8).

I explained that the worship team would come to lead us into worship with an appropriate chorus. Then, at a given point, we would once again sing spontaneously, as we had done often during those days, but during these moments our many personal songs would consist of only one word "holy." We would sing this word, I further suggested, to melodies that would come from each heart individually and yet blend together corporately.

It was to be yet another experiment in intercessory worship, but I was certain the Lord was leading us. As the worship team came, I briefly reminded participants about the cardboard boxes that would be there later in the worship if they felt led to give a gift for the nations, as an act of worship.

Soon we were singing a worshipful chorus that before long led us into a time of spontaneously singing the word "holy." It was difficult for me to tell when the transition initially occurred because the hundreds of participants were singing in Cantonese, the Chinese dialect of Hong Kong.

Suddenly the auditorium was filled with a sound of beauty unlike I had ever heard. Later my wife, Dee, would confirm that she too had heard this heavenly sound. It was as if a new instrument had been created through the voices of these many worshipers.

The sound rose, subsided and rose again. At times, it would be sustained for 10 to 15 minutes, subside and then rise again for an even longer period. I had not specifically suggested that we worship God extravagantly (I am not sure I even knew how), but that was clearly what transpired. This was lavish worship. Like the Latin root for the word "extravagant," everyone seemed to be "wandering outside" the usual limits of worship—if there are such limits. These believers were wandering in lavish worship.

THE EXTRAVAGANCE OF DAVIDIC WORSHIP

But that was not the end of the extravagance. Soon participants were moving toward the cardboard boxes with their gifts. What had started with just a few givers exploded into a display of extravagant sacrificial giving. It seemed that every person participated. Some literally ran with their gifts. Others were dancing before the Lord as they came to a cardboard box.

The worship team, recognizing this spirited worship, began singing a song of celebration. The whole scene reminded me of a journey I had taken into Africa's equatorial rain forest five years earlier, where newly converted pygmies had danced freely before the Lord in worship. They especially loved to dance during the offering time. Offerings in the forest, I was told, often took as much time as the sermon. Pygmies, it was explained, just could not seem to stop dancing. Now Hong Kong was catching this spirit of unrestrained extravagance.

The following morning Agatha excitedly told me the amount of the offering. It was the largest she had ever seen at such a gathering, Hong Kong $390,000 (U.S. $50,000). That morning as she shared the news with conference participants, they applauded with delight. Realizing some participants had missed the Sunday session because it was Easter, Agatha mentioned that additional offering envelopes would be available at the registration table.

The next day as Agatha met us at our hotel to take us to the airport for our trip home, she reported that another Hong Kong $100,000 (almost U.S. $13,000) had been given in those extra envelopes.

It was lavish, unrestrained, exorbitant and fantastic. It was Davidic extravagance! And I suspect that as the spirit of David's Tabernacle is raised globally, we will see much more such extravagance, both in intercessory worship as well as in sacrificial giving.

CHAPTER EIGHT

PATHWAY SIX:
PASSIONATE WORSHIP

WHITE-HOT WORSHIP

It was our regularly scheduled monthly day of prayer at Every Home for Christ. Since becoming the international president in 1988, I have set aside a day each month to join members of our staff to wait on God over ministry issues and for the personal needs of our global full-time staff of some 2,000 workers. We had not missed a month for five years when one of those unique "intercessory moments" occurred.

I define an intercessory moment as one of those occasions when God comes in an unusual way into a prayer gathering and speaks through one of His intercessors. It happened that day, and it significantly impacted a book I had just finished writing at the time, *The Jericho Hour*. In it I describe how it seemed that the Church globally had entered a season of suddenlies, resulting in Jericho-type walls such as Communism in the Soviet Union, Eastern Europe, Ethiopia, etc., falling down right and left. We were, as I suggested, entering the Jericho Hour.[1]

A HEAVENLY INTERRUPTION

As I entered our prayer room that morning, I had the finished manuscript with me—all 220 pages or so—because I wanted the intercessors to pray over it. It is something I do with every manuscript I write before I submit it to a publisher.

Midway through the day, I produced the manuscript and asked each person present to hold it for a few moments and pray for God's blessing as the publishing process began. I explained, as I would usually do on such an occasion, that while their prayers would not actually change the content on a page, they would help prepare the hearts of those who would someday read these pages.

I further explained that editors would study these pages. Their prayers would also help the editors to fine-tune the wording. Having this time of corporate prayer was my way of saying that as far as I was concerned, this book was finished.

Kindly, the intercessors began to pray. Their petitions on my behalf were most encouraging. But a rather interesting thing happened when Tommie Femrite, one of the intercessors, prayed. Tommie had served for years as executive vice president in a ministry called Intercessors International; and whenever she was in town and available, she would join us for these times of prayer. To me, Tommie was as in tune as any intercessor I had ever prayed with. Tommie took my manuscript and began to pray. It was a gracious strategic-level prayer, asking God to use the book to bless Christ's Body throughout the world and to equip readers in the theme of the book.

Then it happened. Tommie stopped her prayer mid-sentence. It initially seemed like the kind of pause a person praying in public sometimes makes when they suddenly lose their train of thought and do not know what to say next. But I quickly realized this was not the case.

"God just spoke to me," Tommie finally said. "Dick, it's about this manuscript." Everyone looked up, including me. We all wondered what Tommie might be hearing.

What she said next gave me heartburn.

"God just told me your book isn't finished yet. It's missing a final chapter!"

For a moment I wondered what on earth Tommie was talking about. After all, it was my book, and I had clearly finished it just that week. I also had told my publisher that it was on its way. My intention was to send it by overnight mail that very day. In fact, I had only kept it so that these intercessors could pray over it.

Tommie softly added, "Dick, there's something to be added about intimacy with God, something God wants to show you about how intimacy is the key to our victory in spiritual warfare."

INTIMACY IN WARFARE

It was, indeed, an intercessory moment. I started to weep—not just cry—but weep. I was the only one on planet Earth, besides God Himself, who knew what Tommie was talking about. I had not even told my wife, Dee.

I had deliberately chosen not to include a chapter in that book which would describe the most intimate, passionate moment I could ever remember in God's presence. I had contemplated telling the story but the concluded readers might think I was a little unbalanced theologically (the word I actually thought was "whacko"!). Now I knew God wanted the experience told.

Within a few days the chapter titled "Warfare Intimacy" (which still seems like an oxymoron) was written. After all, what does warfare have in common with intimacy? Warfare is fighting, and intimacy is loving. I was trying to convey that the key to victory in all of our warfare is our intimacy with God. The encounter did become the subject of that last chapter of *The Jericho Hour,* which I revisit here because of its relationship to the coming restoration of passionate Davidic worship.

In December 1987, I felt a strong directive from the Lord to set aside a month for prayer. I committed to spending my usual office hours in prayer, rather than typical ministry activities.

That experience prepared me to go to the Berlin Wall to pray in January 1988. The journey to Berlin would have profound implications for the ministry I would come to lead, Every Home for Christ, with its sweeping plan to reach every home on earth with the gospel—including all the Eastern Bloc nations, including Russia and the other

14 nations that made up the Soviet Union. At the time all these countries were tightly closed to evangelism of this nature.

As I prayerfully anticipated spending that month in prayer, I wondered if I could actually pray every day as I had intended. To bring variety to the month, it occurred to me that I should set aside certain days for specific focuses. One thought that came to mind was to spend an entire day worshiping the Lord in song with other intercessors.

Singing songs in prayer was not new to me. To sing for an entire day, however, was another matter. Yet, I decided to go through with it.

This day of worship prayer was set for midway through the month. We had numerous volunteer intercessors who came to pray at least weekly at the ministry I then directed, Change the World Ministries. I invited those whom I felt would be comfortable with such extended worship to join me.

About six intercessors came for the entire day; a few others came for shorter time segments. As we began, I explained that we would sing our prayers and praises throughout that day, suggesting that this may have been what Paul had in mind when he spoke of singing "spiritual songs" and "making melody with your heart to the Lord" (see Eph. 5:19, *NASB*).

I also suggested we could sing other worship choruses we knew, but we should not hesitate to sing spontaneously either our own made-up songs or passages from Scripture, such as the psalms, to our own made-up melodies.

A SONG OF INTIMACY

Sometime around the middle of the afternoon one of our staff members, Wes Wilson, began to sing just such a personal song. I think by then each of us there had developed enough courage to sing out, and Wes was no exception.

But as Wes started to sing, I had to hold back a chuckle, wondering where on earth he was going with his made-up lyrics. I held the chuckle back as Wes began to sing, "Lord, our culture has a saying, 'We make our bed and lie in it.'"

Wes paused there momentarily, as if to gather his thoughts for the next phrase. By now I was rather interested in hearing what that phrase might be.

Wes continued, "But, Lord, we have chosen to make for You a bed of song, and we have come with our melodies just to love You."[2]

As strange as the lyrics were, somehow that song touched heaven. Wes is neither a soloist nor a musician, but his song was one of deep personal passion. When he concluded, I continued his theme with my own song. I do not recall a single specific phrase of my song, except that I was expressing a desire to be fully consumed by God. And that is when the heavens opened. It is hard to describe the wonder of the moment. To me, the very presence of God had come.

It was a time of tears and a time of joy. I felt as if God had taken me into His arms and was holding me more lovingly than I have ever been held before. To describe the experience merely as divine romance is terribly inadequate in portraying the passion of the moment. Yet, as is the case in the intimacy of marriage when seeds of conception are planted that ultimately lead to birth, I felt as if something was conceived during those moments of intimacy.

Late that afternoon I went home and decided to spend a few more quiet moments in our backyard prayer chapel (actually, it's a shed that has been turned into a glorified prayer closet!). Sitting quietly and meditating, I could not get that picture of conception out of my mind. *Something has been conceived today*, I said repeatedly to myself.

As I sat there, I glanced at the new 1988 calendar I had tacked up on the wall and thought about the coming year.

I thought of the process of birth in humans—how it takes nine months from conception to birth. Once again I thought, *Something has been conceived today!*

So I took the calendar and began counting the days— nine month's worth—flipping each page in the process. It ended on September 12, 1988. I took a felt-tip marker and wrote in the blank space for that day: "Something will be born today."

At the time I wrote those words, I directed a prayer-mobilization ministry called Change the World Ministries. Little could I have known that within eight months the board of directors of Every Home for Christ would prayerfully approach me to lead their much larger global ministry, which at that time had major campaigns in more than 70 nations.

After several months of planning and discussing— with much prayer—Every Home for Christ's board of directors officially appointed me to the position of international president. Board Chairman Andy Duda notified me of their decision on September 1, 1988.

I thought that perhaps I would have at least several months to transition into this new role, but God had other plans. He had a date to keep!

That first day in September, as I spoke by phone with

Andy Duda, I asked him when he felt I should assume this new position.

"Could you possibly begin a week from Monday?" Andy responded, a little hesitantly. EHC had been without a president for more than a year, and the board was anxious to move forward quickly.

"Let's see," I said, as I reached for my small pocket calendar. "That would be . . . September 12!" God does, indeed, keep His dates!

Something clearly remarkable was born in my life on that day of intimate worship, and it has radically impacted every day since. In fact, as of the time of this writing, Every Home for Christ has conducted home-to-home evangelism campaigns in well over 100 nations, with many thousands of full-time and volunteer evangelism teams having visited more than 225 million homes—all since that day in 1988. It seemed the intimacy of that unusual day of singing in 1987 had indeed conceived in my life more than I could ever have imagined. And to me, I am now more certain than ever, it is all a part of David's Tabernacle being restored.

THE FOUNDATION OF A TABERNACLE

Through that unique birthing experience that began in 1987, God was already laying a foundation in my heart regarding the coming restoration of David's Tabernacle, even though at the time I never saw the link between the Acts 15:16-18 prophecy and the harvest of Gentiles (non-Jewish people groups) that Every Home for Christ was so involved in.

> Passion for God and passion for God's purposes in transforming peoples and nations go hand in hand.

Passion, I was to learn, was the key—passion for God and passion for God's purposes in transforming peoples and nations go hand in hand. Consider the wise words of John Piper: "When the flame of worship burns with the heat of God's true worth, the light of missions will shine to the most remote peoples on earth. Where passion for God is weak, the zeal for missions will be weak."[3]

Passion was written all over David's Tabernacle and everything else about Davidic worship. The white-hot flame of worship never went out during David's watch. If the spirit of David's Tabernacle is to be restored globally, then that flame will surely spread, igniting a passion for God's presence everywhere.

Consider some of the songs David sang to the Lord. We know them as psalms. They are wildly passionate. David sings, "My whole being will exclaim, 'Who is like you, O LORD?'" (Ps. 35:10).

How does one's whole being exalt God? This was clearly David's desire and he pursued it with a passion.

On another occasion David demonstrated this passion when he sang, "Passion for your house burns within me" (Ps. 69:9, *NLT*). Here, again, we find an expression of David's desire for intimacy with the Father. David is a man obsessed and absolutely abandoned to God.

Many centuries later Madame Guyon would describe such a person: "Our Lord is very jealous over any saint who is utterly abandoned to Him. He does not let that believer have any pleasures at all outside of Himself."[4]

BUMPING INTO BUILDINGS

Such a worshiper was David. He once likened his passion for God's presence to that of a deer desperately thirsting for water. We recall his song, "As the deer pants for streams of water, so my soul pants for you, O God. My soul thirsts for God, for the living God. When can I go and meet with God?" (Ps. 42:1-2). What amazing passion! It is all consuming.

Later King David would sing, "How lovely is your dwelling place, O LORD Almighty. I long, yes, I faint with longing to enter the courts of the LORD. With my whole being, body and soul, I will shout joyfully to the living God" (Ps. 84:1-2, *NLT*).

> David's passion for God never seemed to lose that all-consuming fervency and neither should ours.

Here we see something of the passion one experiences when falling in love. But David's passion was not a passing infatuation; it was a longing that consumed him throughout his life.

I recall, sometimes humorously, that season of life decades ago when I fell in love with my wife, Dee. I would bump into buildings I did not see, trip over things on the sidewalk that were not there and even forget to eat. I was a basket case of love.

Over the years, of course, I have recultivated that ability to eat and am now able to walk quite well without bumping into buildings or tripping over things that are not there—all while still loving my wife deeply. Ours is a love that has matured into a rich companionship.

David's passion for God, however, never seemed to lose that all-consuming emotional fervency, and neither should ours. We should always be, like David, hopelessly and passionately in love with the Father.

We see this almost desperate passion in one of David's most memorable songs, Psalm 63. Here David pleads,

> O God, you are my God; I earnestly search for you. My soul thirsts for you; my whole body longs for you in this parched and weary land where there is no water. I have seen you in your sanctuary and gazed upon your power and glory. Your unfailing love is better to me than life itself; how I praise you! I will honor you as long as I live, lifting up my hands to you in prayer. You satisfy me more than the richest of foods. I will praise you with songs of joy (vv. 1-5, *NLT*).

If the spirit of Davidic worship is to be restored in the last days, we can expect it to include a fervency of passion perhaps unlike the Church has ever seen. We will all be bumping into buildings (the house of God, no doubt) and forgetting to eat (as we frequently fast and worship). And God, indeed, will satisfy us more than the richest of foods! Are you getting hungry?

PATHWAY SEVEN:
EXPRESSIVE WORSHIP
TO DANCE OR DIE

"This may be hard for some to admit," A. W. Tozer taught, "but when we are truly worshiping and adoring the God of all grace and of all love and of all mercy and of all truth, we may not be quiet enough to please everyone."[1]

At David's Tabernacle we see no absence of exuberance. Silence has its place, and elsewhere in my writings on intercessory worship I have built a case for more of it (see *Heights of Delight*, chapter 3). But we miss something vital about David's Tabernacle if we fail to see the expressive nature of its worship. Look again at this description of the Ark being brought from Gibeon into David's tent:

> David, wearing a linen ephod, danced before the Lord with all his might, while he and the entire house of Israel brought up the ark of the Lord with shouts and the sound of trumpets. As the ark of the Lord was entering the City of David, Michal daughter of Saul watched from a window. And when she saw King David leaping and dancing before the Lord, she despised him in her heart (2 Sam. 6:14-16).

Another account tells us:

> But as the Ark of the Lord's covenant entered the City of David, Michal, the daughter of Saul, looked down from her window. When she saw King David dancing and leaping for joy, she was filled with contempt for him (1 Chron. 15:29, NLT).

DRIVEN BY DELIGHT

Although there is a vital lesson to be dealt with later about the sad reaction of David's wife, Michal, to the king's worship intensity, here I simply want to highlight David's exuberance. He was "dancing and leaping for joy" (v. 29, *NLT*). The account in 2 Samuel 6 tells us David "danced before the LORD with all his might" (v. 14, *NLT*). He put all his emotion into his worship.

This emotion-driven expressiveness is seen on numerous occasions of David's worship. Once David sang, "No wonder my heart is filled with joy, and my mouth shouts his praises!" (Ps. 16:9, *NLT*). David's worship was clearly driven by his sheer delight in God.

On another occasion, David admonished, "Sing praises to God and to his name! Sing loud praises to him who rides the clouds. His name is the LORD—rejoice in his presence!" (Ps. 68:4, *NLT*).

David was into *loud!* He told of offering sacrifices in his Tabernacle with "shouts of joy" (Ps. 27:6) and instructed musicians to praise God with "loud clanging cymbals" (Ps. 150:5, *NLT*).

Some might say that all that emotion was just a cultural thing—the Hebrew way of worshiping. Jack

Hayford deals with this argument in his book *Worship His Majesty*. Regarding expressive worship, Hayford suggested, "Opponents of expressive worship will occasionally concede the New Testament does contain a few references to forthright, open praise. Still, the presumption is that expressiveness in worship went out with the blood-sacrifice system or that such unabashed physical exuberance was only a cultural trait passed down by Hebrew tradition."[2]

Hayford goes on to correct this fallacy, explaining that the essence of sacrifice never really left worship, and it never will. He cites the author of Hebrews, "Therefore by Him let us continually offer the sacrifice of praise to God, that is, the fruit of our lips, giving thanks to His name" (Heb. 13:15, *NKJV*).

Jack Hayford then concludes, "The New Testament contains more direct references to expressive worship than usually meet the eye. Singing, praising, up-raised voices, lifting hands, kneeling, offerings and reading of the Scriptures are all mentioned. (See Luke 24:50; Acts 2:46-47; 4:24; 20:36; 1 Corinthians 14:15; 16:1-3; 1 Timothy 2:8; 2 Timothy 2:15)."[3]

Worship related to David's tent clearly was expressive. If we are to see a significant restoration of such worship in the last days, we should not be surprised by a growing movement of exuberant praise.

It certainly will not shock God. Joseph Garlington comments, "If the experiences of King David are any guide, God likes exuberant and elaborate praise with lots of dancing and excitement, and enough instruments to reach every eardrum for miles."[4]

WHIRLING IN WORSHIP

Dancing as a form of expressive worship is one example of exuberant praise that is growing among churches world-wide. I believe it is a sign of at least the beginning of David's Tabernacle being restored. Perhaps a brief biblical background regarding dancing would be in order.

When Miriam and other Israeli women sang and danced before the Lord following the miracle at the Red Sea (see Exod. 15:20-21), the Hebrew word used for "dance" is *mecholah*, whose other form, *machowl*, means "a round dance."[5]

When David danced before the Lord as the Ark was brought into his tent (see 2 Sam. 6:14-16), the Hebrew word used is *karar*. It means "to dance, to whirl about."[6] In a parallel account of this event where David dances before the Ark, the word used for "dance" is *raqad*, meaning "to stomp or to spring about wildly for joy."[7] "Raqad" is variously translated "dance, jump, leap, skip" (see 1 Chron. 15:29).

The use of two different Hebrew words to describe the same event may suggest a combination of these expressions. Can you picture King David leaping and stomping, jumping and skipping, as he whirls about wildly in worship?

Interestingly, the word "rejoice," in Greek *agalliao*, similarly means "to jump for joy"[8] (see 1 Pet. 1:6,8; Rev. 19:7). It is derived from the Greek words *agan*, meaning "much," and *hallomai*, meaning "to jump, leap or spring up."

Thus, "agalliao" literally means "to jump or leap." According to a Bible concordance, it would properly be translated "to jump for joy." This suggests that even in the New Testament we see expressiveness by those who encounter the Lord.

This is not to suggest that all worship *must* involve such ecstatic expressions, but neither should we reject or avoid them. Feelings can be a vital part of worship. A. W. Tozer once wrote, "I have had people tell me very dogmatically that they will never allow 'feeling' to have any part of their spiritual life and experience. I reply, 'Too bad for you!'" That wise worshiper continued, "I say that because I have voiced a very real definition of what I believe worship to be: *worship is to feel in the heart!*"[9]

Tozer carefully cautions those who would avoid any feelings in worship. He wrote:

> If you wake up tomorrow morning and there is absolute numbness in your right arm—no feeling at all—you will quickly dial the doctor with your good left hand. Real worship is, among other things, a feeling about our God. It is in our hearts. And we must be willing to express it in an appropriate manner.[10]

Of course, Tozer's appropriate manner is open to question, usually based on one's theology, personality or even culture; however, his point is well taken: Worship should involve our feelings.

SHEDDING OUR DIGNITY

"You can't preserve your dignity and see His Deity," Tommy Tenney wrote. "You can't save your face and seek His face."[11]

Often we quote Scripture in such a way as to suggest some kind of a standard for so-called dignified worship. As Joseph Garlington suggests, we tend to overlook vast biblical references to exuberant praise and quote passages such as Habakkuk 2:20, "But the LORD is in his holy temple; let all the earth be silent before him." Of these words Garlington says, "Somehow this isolated verse has been elevated to the level of a church doctrine or ordinance of operation. The truth is that this verse is almost always quoted with no reference to context."[12]

Let's look more carefully at the full text and we will see what Garlington means:

> Woe to him who says to a piece of wood, "Awake!" To a dumb stone, "Arise!" And that is your teacher? Behold, it is overlaid with gold and silver, and there is no breath at all inside it. But the LORD is in His holy temple. Let all the earth be silent before Him. A prayer of Habakkuk the prophet, according to Shigionoth. LORD, I have heard the report about Thee and I fear. O Lord, revive Thy work in the midst of the years, in the midst of the years make it known; in wrath remember mercy (Hab. 2:19–3:2, *NASB*).

For one thing, the directive in this passage is for all the earth to be silent, not specifically God's people (even though someone might suggest that all the earth would include God's people). Further, this is also said in a context condemning idolatry; idols that have "no breath at all."

But there is something else of special significance in this passage. It is an interesting Hebrew word that we usually skip over (or, as in my case, mispronounce), especially if we are reading the passage publicly. So, we highlight "Let all the earth be silent," and leave out "A prayer of Habakkuk the prophet, according to Shigionoth" (Hab. 3:1).

True, we sometimes leave this expression out because it starts another chapter (even though chapter numbers were not in the original text) and also because it seems like some kind of instructive note—which it is.

"Shigionoth" is a musical or literary term. The *New Living Translation* renders the phrase simply, "This prayer was sung by the prophet Habakkuk" (Hab. 3:1).

The Amplified Bible comes even closer to the heart and depth of the term. It reads, "A prayer of Habakkuk the prophet, set to wild, enthusiastic, and triumphal music" (Hab. 3:1).

CHAPTER NINE

HALLELUJAH ANYWAY!

Years ago, I recall hearing the story of a little Scottish woman, probably in her 80s, who attended a small church in the Highlands. She was often expressive in her worship and for years had had a rather tolerant pastor who forgave a periodic emotion-driven "Amen" or "Hallelujah."

That pastor eventually moved away and another came to their community to replace him. Far more reserved, the new rector found the lady's outbursts deeply troubling. His hair would bristle, his throat would become dry, and he would often lose his place in his sermon.

After spending only a month or two in the pulpit and hearing the woman shout "Hallelujah" one too many times, the reverend approached the elderly saint. He decided to make her an offer. Knowing the woman had little by way of worldly possessions, he offered her a brand-new, beautiful wool blanket if only she could sit and remain silent through a month of services. The little lady knew how desperately she could use that wool blanket, so she decided to give it a try.

She made it through the first two Sundays, but it was not easy. She even suspected the pastor was deliberately trying to be dull just to help her out. Several times she almost slipped, but she would plant her feet, clench her teeth and force herself to listen in silence.

The third Sunday the saint sat stone-faced, staring at a stained-glass window and imagining the warmth of that new wool blanket. But her mind had wandered just a little too far, and by the time she was able to collect her thoughts, she forgot where she was. The preacher said something uncharacteristically inspiring and the little lady lost it! Leaping to her feet and waving her hands wildly in the air, the old saint shouted, "Blanket or no blanket, hallelujah anyway!"

JOINING THE DANCE

As Davidic-type worship is restored in the last days, it may include a few such interruptions. David danced expressively—even wildly—because he could not help himself. He interrupted the processional as the Ark was coming and danced with ecstatic delight.

A sad and tragic endnote to the occasion is the response of David's wife, Michal. She watched from a distance, behind closed doors. Why she was not with the worshipers is a fair question.

The Bible says she "despised [David] in her heart!" (1 Chron. 15:29). Michal's motivation is mystifying; her behavior baffling. The text does not fully address the reason behind her reaction, but the fruit of her bitterness is made clear: She would be barren for life (see 2 Sam. 6:23).

As David's tabernacle of intercessory worship is restored, we will face this question: Do we dance like David or despise like Michal? Said another way: Do we dance or die? The fruit to be gained or lost will be the fruit of the harvest.

Do you feel like dancing?

PATHWAY EIGHT:
OPEN WORSHIP

A BREAK WITH PRIESTLY PROTOCOL

A fascinating observation about David's Tabernacle, implied by much of the context surrounding it, is that the tent was open for public view.

Of David's Tabernacle, and the Ark it housed, Mike Bickle wrote, "A tabernacle is a portable shrine. The tabernacle of David . . . was a small tent—only about 10 or 15 feet high and long (1 Chronicles 15:1; 16:1). The glory of God rested on the Ark, yet it was enshrined in a simple tent."[1]

Bickle adds, "In Moses' time, the glory that rested on the Ark was well hidden in the Holy of Holies, behind a thick veil. In David's tent, there was no veil to keep the people from seeing the glory of God. It was completely unprecedented—David laid the Ark of the Covenant in open view."[2]

We reach this conclusion of an open tent by inference from the context of the tent being first set up in Jerusalem and the Ark being brought in. Notice this biblical description of those final moments of the Ark being brought from Gibeon to Jerusalem:

> So they brought the Ark of God into the special tent David had prepared for it, and they sacrificed burnt offerings and peace offerings *before God*. David appointed the following Levites to lead the people in worship *before the Ark of the LORD* by asking for his blessings and giving thanks and praise to the LORD, the God of Israel (1 Chron. 16:1,4, *NLT*; emphasis added).

Two expressions here are vital—"before God" and "before the Ark of the Lord." There is nothing here that suggests the Ark was hidden as it was in Moses' day.

NO NEED FOR BELLS

At Moses' tabernacle, the Ark was well hidden—concealed behind a thick veil in the holy of holies. Only the high priest could enter that special place—and then only once a year.

We recall that Moses' tabernacle had three specific areas: the outer court, the inner court (the holy place) and the most holy place (the holy of holies). There was a large veil or tapestry that separated the holy place from the holy of holies, which prevented both access and view by anyone except the high priest.

David radically changes all this. It was not a mere paradigm shift—it was more of a tectonic shift. Spiritually speaking, it was of earthquake proportions.

Now we see the Levites ministering directly before the Ark continuously. And all of the people, as our text declares, join them "in worship before the Ark" (v. 4, *NLT*).

Joseph Garlington uniquely describes this openness: "The holy Ark of the covenant was simply covered with a tent—it was not blocked or concealed from view. The tent was only extensive enough to protect the Ark from natural elements like rain, heavy dew, and the sun's rays." Garlington adds, "If you remember, the Tabernacle of

Moses had three layers of a shielding separating the Shekinah presence of God from the common people."[3]

There was something different about David when it came to a worship protocol. He enjoyed radical worship. He did not just march to the beat of a different drummer, he danced to the beat of his own drum—his heart pounding passionately after God. And in all this, he seems to have wanted everyone to join him.

David was a worship leader who had a side job as king. Once he sang to the Lord, "I will thank you in front of the entire congregation. I will praise you before all the people" (Ps. 35:18, *NLT*). David led the way in worship.

It is easy sometimes to read through our Bibles and miss simple statements of profound significance. A brief phrase in 2 Samuel 7:18 falls into this category. We read, "David went in and sat before the LORD." No big deal, we might say—except for the fact of who David was and where he sat down.

David was in God's presence, in His tent. He was sitting in front of the Ark. Yet David was neither a priest nor a Levite. Under Jewish law only a Levite could minister in this holy place, and only the high priest could go into the holy of holies to minister before the Ark. Further, the high priest did not sit, he stood—and he kept moving. The sounds of the bells on his garment signaled all was well (see Exod. 28:33-35).

David? He just sits there, carrying on a conversation with God. He had no need for bells. Of this break with priestly protocol, Joseph Garlington writes, "What we see here is that David represents a greater priesthood, a type and shadow of the coming Messiah, which is confirmed in Hebrews 7:12-16."[4]

Garlington adds, "David was unknowingly demonstrating that a greater priesthood was coming, a priesthood rooted in worship, not mere ritual or ancestral lineage." The author concludes, "We have become a kingdom of priests and kings in Christ before God. David was a type and shadow of the better priesthood to come."[5]

A LOOK PAST THE VEIL

David seemed to break all the rules set by those who preceded him. This man after God's own heart wanted everyone to catch a glimpse of the heart of God. I believe he intentionally kept the tent open—and God allowed it. Some 1,000 years before Christ would die on the cross and the veil in the temple would be permanently split in half,

He allowed David to briefly lift the veil for a relatively short preresurrection view.

Concerning that very veil, and David's apparent exemption from being required to use it, Tommy Tenney suggests, "God never did like the veil. He had to have it, but he didn't like it. When Jesus died on the cross at Calvary, God was the one who ripped the veil from top to bottom in the temple of Herod in Jerusalem. He ripped it in such a way that it could never be rewoven again." Tenney concludes, "David's tabernacle was the only one of any of these structures [i.e., Moses' Tabernacle, David's tent, Solomon's Temple] that had no veil."[6]

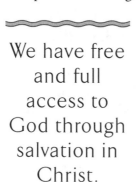

We have free and full access to God through salvation in Christ.

Why was David apparently given this veil exemption? Mike Bickle suggests that God allowed the worshipers themselves (some 4,000 musicians plus 288 singers) to replace the veil for that particular season (see 1 Chron. 6:31-32; 15:16-24; 23:4-19). Bickle writes, "Instead of the thick veil Moses used, David made musicians and singers into a human veil around the Ark."[7]

Although we know now that this veil has been lifted and we have free and full access to God through salvation in Christ, one wonders if we understand fully the totality of this access. It is for us much more than a one-time visit, even though Christ's sacrifice was indeed "once for all" (Heb. 9:26). Similarly, our personal salvation happens just once. But I am speaking here of taking advantage of the removed veil through daily, passionate worship.

ASLEEP THROUGH THE GLORY

Not long ago my wife and I were flying to Hong Kong from Chicago in a jumbo jet packed with some 400 passengers. That day we were taking the polar route (which would take us almost directly over the North Pole and save us a couple hours of flying).

Long-range air travel has significantly improved since our first missions trip in 1966 to British Honduras on a sputtering propeller-driven DC-3. Today, individual television screens pop up from your seat, and on those 12- to 14-hour flights some people watch one movie after another to pass the hours.

I am more interested in the trip map that appears continuously on one channel of the video. It is fascinating.

It constantly shows you exactly where you are with a tiny silhouette of an airplane over an ever-changing map. At intervals of about every 30 seconds the screen will also show you the airspeed, the time at your destination, how long it will take to get to your destination and the plane's altitude.

Strangely, it also tells you the outside temperature, which is usually about 50 to 60 degrees below zero. I suppose they show you this so that you will be thankful for the barely survivable cabin temperature you are feeling, hoping that you will not complain of it being horribly hot or unbelievably cold.

Wow! you say to yourself. *It may be nearly 110 degrees here in the cabin, but that's better than 50 degrees below zero outside.*

We were about eight hours into the flight and everyone around me, Dee included, was asleep. I popped open the in-seat video console and pushed the channel number for the trip map.

We're right on top of the North Pole, I thought. Judging from the tiny blip of the plane on the map, and the speed the map said we were traveling, I figured we were about 40 minutes or so from passing as near to the North Pole as you can get without messing up the cockpit compass bigtime. At perfect north, we are told, everything is south, so plane compasses and gyroscopes go nuts. To avoid this problem, planes do not fly exactly over the pole.

I noticed that two rows behind us and on the other side of the cabin there was an empty row of seats, right by the window, on our otherwise packed flight. I decided to go back and take a look out the window. Even though it was nighttime for us, it was broad daylight outside, because at that time of the year it was constant daylight at the North Pole. Thus, all the window shades were closed and virtually everyone on board was asleep.

Slowly and somewhat reluctantly, I lifted the shade. I was afraid the bright sunlight would wake everyone in the cabin, but my fears subsided as the light began to enter and no one stirred. They were all more exhausted than I had thought.

As I looked down, I began to see sights I had never before seen. It was magnificent. Sweeping dunes of brilliant white snow and snow cliffs that must have been 200 feet high could be seen so clearly from such a distance. I watched with rapt attention and could not take my eyes off the glorious landscape.

I popped the video console up at the seat I had moved to and checked the trip map again. We were as close to the North Pole as we would pass.

I looked down out of the window and could not believe what I saw. It was an arctic station of some kind. The numerous tiny quonset huts were clearly visible. *Goodness*, I thought, *that's the famous scientific outpost at the North Pole. You can't get closer than that.*

I looked around to see if others had shared in this mesmerizing moment. Amazingly, not another window shade was open. The entire polar landscape had passed in all its wonder and everyone else missed it. It was veiled from each by a simple window shade—and a desire for sleep. I remember praying at that moment, "O God, please don't let me ever sleep through Your glory. Don't let any veil keep me from Your presence."

OPEN TO SAVIOR-SENSITIVE WORSHIP

Davidic worship seeks to remind us that the veil is still removed. The tent curtains are up. We should not be afraid of open worship. To a degree, I can understand the seeker-sensitive mentality that in some church-growth models intends to create a comfort level for newcomers. Yet, we should not fear a Savior-sensitive worship model either, one that seeks to create a climate for the Lord

Himself to come—and act! I believe it is possible to have both.

A worship mentor for many people, Jack Hayford illustrated this balance for more than 25 years during his leadership as senior pastor at The Church on the Way in Van Nuys, California. My wife and I had the joy of attending Jack's church for more than a decade while Every Home for Christ was headquartered in the Los Angeles area.

We discovered quickly that The Church on the Way was a fellowship built on worship. Though we felt more fed from the Word during those years than at any previous church, what we remember most was the open, sustained, focused worship. From the outset of a service, everyone worshiped. Hands would be lifted everywhere in praise as if a giant magnet of sorts swept over the congregation pulling everyone's arms skyward. Dee and I had not been used to this totality of wor-

> Davidic worship seeks to remind us that the veil is removed. The tent curtains are up. We should not be afraid of open worship.

ship previously, but we quickly entered in with delight.

During these days something unique happened to my wife, and God used it to demonstrate to me the power of open praise. At the time, we lived in the Santa Clarita Valley of the Los Angeles area, a good distance from The Church on the Way, which was located in a neighboring valley, the San Fernando Valley. We considered the drive well worth it for the worship and the Word.

I mention the distance we traveled because it had some bearing on my wife's unusual experience. Dee had been to a nearby beauty salon for a perm and that evening shared something I thought was a little odd, something concerning a conversation that she had had that day with her beautician.

As Dee's perm was finishing, her hairdresser had asked about my occupation. My wife responded simply, "Dick is a minister."

Not realizing that some ministers may not be pastors of congregations, the woman responded, "Oh, that's wonderful, Mrs. Eastman. What church does your husband serve as a minister?"

Because my wife was now paying for her perm and in a hurry to get to another appointment, she refrained from giving the lady a lengthy explanation about the ministry I then directed. Instead, she said simply, "Oh, we go to a church called The Church on the Way."

Dee's hairdresser raised her head and with a look of both shock and joy said, "Oh, Mrs. Eastman, that's wonderful. I can't believe it. Oh, this is so exciting. I just can't believe that, Mrs. Eastman. What wonderful news!"

Dee was obviously startled by her response and commented, "I didn't know you attended our church."

"Oh, I don't go to any church, Mrs. Eastman," the lady explained. "In fact, I've never been to an actual church service in my life—only to funerals or weddings."

The woman could tell Dee was moderately confused. How could someone be so excited about a church that she had never visited—especially someone who did not attend any church and never had?

Dee's hairdresser quickly added, "I guess I should explain why I'm so excited about your church."

The woman then shared briefly about her bouts of discouragement and depression and that many days she wondered if she could make it. Then, just a few days earlier, a client began to tell her about the change in her own life that healed her of similar oppression. It all began when the client had found a church in the San Fernando Valley called The Church on the Way. It was there, the client explained, that she had found Christ as Savior.

Dee's hairdresser's eyes filled with tears as she added, "Mrs. Eastman, the reason I'm so excited is this Sunday I get to go to your church, and I can't wait."

FAITH BY ANTICIPATION

Dee chuckled as she told me what had happened. "Isn't it amazing," she said, "that someone who never attends church can be so excited, even though she's never been there before?" *That's a different kind of faith,* I thought—*faith by anticipation!*

I am not sure I would even have remembered that conversation had it not been for what happened the following Sunday.

We arrived for church at least 45 minutes (perhaps an hour) before the third service that morning, hoping to get a seat in the main sanctuary (which at the time held about 700).

Each Sunday had five identical services, but this still did not adequately handle the crowds. If you were merely on time (or, heaven forbid, late), you would be ushered down a dark stairway into one of several auxiliary rooms where you could watch the worship and hear the Word on a small-screen television. I jokingly called it "ant worship" because Pastor Jack and the other pastors looked like ants.

Even if you did get there in plenty of time, there would typically be people already standing in incredibly long lines that wrapped around the building and stretched down a side street. So once in line, you still had to dig in, in a quasi-Christian military manner, to protect your position. When the doors actually opened, these lines of nice people seemed to melt into a human free-for-all, each person struggling for a place just a little farther ahead in line.

To this day, my memory of the doors opening is that of a giant vacuum cleaner sucking in people.

Some, trying to gain an advantage and holding family Bibles (of the size you do not even read at home because they are just too big to comfortably hold), would say "God bless you, brother" to someone standing in front of them and then, as if by accident, pretend to stumble. Using their Bible as a weapon of sorts (not in the sense of Paul's admonishment in Ephesians 6:17), they would push that person back three places in line. I got pretty good at it myself, even with my much smaller but still adequate *Thompson Chain-Reference Bible*.

OPEN HEAVEN THROUGH WORSHIP

Suddenly, the doors opened, the jostling began and the giant vacuum began sucking in people. I was ready to rejoice merely because we had made it into the main sanctuary. *No "ant worship" today,* I thought.

Just then two things happened simultaneously. While Pastor Jack headed toward the microphone to begin a worship chorus, Dee poked me forcefully to get my attention.

"Look," Dee said excitedly, "over there by the pillar." She was nodding her head as inconspicuously as possible toward one of the several pillars scattered throughout the sanctuary.

"The lady in the yellow dress, just left of that pillar," Dee explained, "that's my hairdresser. She's here—in our service! I don't believe it!"

The opening phrases of the chorus were now being sung and, as was typical for worship at The Church on the Way, hands began to go up everywhere. It was a slow worshipful chorus I recall to this day—"In My Life, Lord, Be Glorified!"

As Dee nodded in the direction of her hairdresser, I remembered her telling me four days earlier that the woman had never gone to church anywhere. Naturally I wondered what her reaction would be. So, as I worshiped, I peeked. What I saw next moves me to this day.

Because of the layout of the sanctuary, the row where Dee's hairdresser stood was on an angle in front of us and to the right. This meant I could see her facial expressions clearly, at least from the side. But that really did not matter because shortly she turned her face right in my direction.

First, I saw her mouth drop open in an amazed sort of look, with her eyes still wide open. It takes longer to tell the story than it took to actually happen. The woman looked to the left, then to the right, and then up toward heaven. It was a jerky motion. Then, she shot up one hand and then the other. I had the sense that she was inwardly saying, *Well, if this is how they do it, I'll do it this way, too.*

With her eyes still wide open and both hands raised, I saw two black parallel lines move visibly down from her eyes: mascara was flowing freely with her tears. Gobs of it! Later I would learn that in those brief moments, not more than five minutes into the service, Dee's hairdresser had surrendered her life to Jesus. Worship had not frightened her away nor turned her off.

To Dee's beautician, open worship had been an open invitation to an open heaven. Worship at David's tent was open, and David's kingdom was vastly multiplied as a result. Cultivating a climate of open worship, I believe, will help hasten the restoration of David's fallen tent (Acts 15:16-18) and soften hearts for history's greatest harvest.

Savior-sensitivity will be a vital key, and open worship is clearly Savior-sensitive.

PATHWAY NINE:
PRIMARY WORSHIP
THE MAIN THING

When Brother Lawrence, a radical seventeenth-century monk, was on his deathbed, he used the occasion to preach his lifelong worship message to fellow monks gathered about him:

> "I am not dying," Lawrence told them. "I'm just doing what I have been doing for the past 40 years, and doing what I expect to be doing for all eternity."

"What is that?" a monk asked.

Brother Lawrence answered, "I am worshiping the God I love!"[1]

Commenting on this passionate worshiper's dying words, A. W. Tozer said, "Worshiping God—that was primary for Brother Lawrence. He was also dying, but that was secondary."[2]

It is clear from even the most casual study of David's Tabernacle that the worship surrounding it was not an auxiliary function. It was the absolute priority. Worship was primary. That familiar admonition on establishing priorities— keep the main thing the main thing—especially applied to Davidic worship. In David's House, worship was the main thing!

THE PRIMACY OF WORSHIP

Much of what we refer to as "worship" today, particularly in church-service settings, is too often viewed as the introduction to what happens later in a service. How frequently have you heard the expression, "Worship prepares a way for the Word"?

This is not to suggest the preaching of the Word is insignificant. It is definitely true that worship does create an atmosphere that enhances preaching. But we need to recognize that worship is not merely a stepping-stone to something else: Worship is that something else! Until we grasp this, we miss the whole purpose of God's Word.

The supreme purpose for which God has given us His Word is to direct us toward Himself. Even Jesus, the Living Word, points us to the Father (see John 5:19,30; 6:38; 12:49).

> Worship is not merely a stepping-stone to something else: Worship is that something else!

God is primary in all that relates to eternity. John Piper hammers home this reality in his book *Let the Nations Be Glad*:

God is the absolute reality that everyone in the universe must come to terms with. Everything depends utterly on His will. All other realities compare to Him like a raindrop compares to the ocean, or like an anthill compares to Mount Everest. . . . The most crucial issue in missions is the centrality of God in the life of

the church. Missions is not first and ultimate:
God is.[3]

Of course, it is worship that highlights the centrality
of God. Piper expands these thoughts on the primacy of
God and, thus, the primacy of worship, with a call to clar-
ity of focus regarding this issue. He concludes:

> When the glory of God Himself saturates our
> preaching and teaching and conversation and writ-
> ings, and when He predominates above our talk of
> methods and strategies and psychological buzz
> words and cultural trends, then the people might
> begin to feel that He is the central reality of their
> lives and that the spread of His glory is more impor-
> tant than all their possessions and all their plans.[4]

David, in setting up his tent on Mount Zion, understood this. God was primary; therefore, worship was primary. Indeed, when we look at worship during David's
day, we see just how essential it was. After the Ark was
placed in the tent of David and plans were made to build
a permanent temple for the Ark, we clearly see the primacy of Davidic worship.

Note this description of the praise force David established:

> All the Levites who were thirty years old or older were counted, and the total came to thirty-eight thousand. Then David said, "Twenty-four thousand of them will supervise the work at the Temple of the LORD. Six thousand are to serve as officials and judges. Four thousand will work as gatekeepers, and another four thousand will praise the LORD with the musical instruments I have made" (1 Chron. 23:3-5, *NLT*).

Here we discover that of the entire workforce supervising the building of the temple (38,000), more than 10 percent (4,000) were there to sustain continuous worship. The fact that such a sizable force was assigned to the specific task of worshiping the Lord day and night shows that worship was primary in David's thinking.

This primacy of worship is further emphasized later in this same chapter:

> And each morning and evening they stood before the LORD to sing songs of thanks and

praise to him. They assisted with the burnt offerings that were presented to the LORD on Sabbath days, at new moon celebrations, and at all the appointed festivals. The proper number of Levites served in the LORD's presence at all times, following all the procedures they had been given (1 Chron. 23:30-31, *NLT*).

Here, again, we see how praise and worship in David's day was primary. Focused praise and thanksgiving started and ended each day in a concerted, corporate way. Other ministry to the Lord, such as sacrifices and offerings, also continued at all times, just as the passage describes.

The priority of worship is also seen in an earlier passage of 1 Chronicles where we read, "The musicians, all prominent Levites, lived at the Temple. They were exempt from other responsibilities there since they were on duty at all hours" (9:33, *NLT*).

THE PRIORITY OF WORSHIP

Elsewhere in these chronicles of Israel's ancient kings, we read of the apparent intensive training offered to prepare those who would lead this worship. Notice this description of the 288 specialized worship leaders, "They and their families were all trained in making music before the LORD, and each of them—288 in all—was an accomplished musician" (1 Chron. 25:7, *NLT*). The fact that highly trained musicians and worshipers were on duty at all hours is a clear indication of the priority given to this ministry unto the Lord. This is something demonstrated in all that David did.

Look again at the expression of David's life's purpose as described in one of his most memorable psalms, "One thing I have desired of the LORD, that will I seek: that I may dwell in the house of the LORD all the days of my life, to behold the beauty of the LORD, and to inquire in His temple" (Ps. 27:4, *NKJV*). Few passages in all the Bible better demonstrate the establishing of a personal worship priority than these words of David.

Worship was so foundational to David's life that this king would be content to spend all his days before the Lord in His house. We know from the rest of Psalm 27 that David is referring here to the Tabernacle he had set up on Mount Zion. This was David's tent! In this same psalm he declares, "At his tabernacle will I sacrifice with shouts of joy" (Ps. 27:6, *NIV*).

David's worship desire, as stated in Psalm 27:4, was twofold. First, he wanted to spend priority time in the

Lord's house simply "to behold the beauty of the LORD." He wanted to saturate himself in God. David was a king consumed with God! He wanted to see the Lord in all His splendor—just to be with Him.

Notice how the passage begins: "One thing I have desired." Worship, to David, was primary. Being king was secondary. More than anything else on Earth, this seeking psalmist wanted to experience the glory of the Lord.

Second, David wanted to learn all he could from these worship encounters. All worshipers are true learners. Rare is the genuine worshiper who does not passionately pursue God through His Word daily. It is an interesting fact that over the generations, those who most gave themselves to worshiping the Lord, seemed to know the most about Him. In fact, there seems to be a clear linkage between worship and our understanding of God's Word. Said another way, worshipers are more inclined to inquire in God's temple than believers who worship the Lord little.

THE PRACTICAL POWER OF WORSHIP

Jack Hayford highlights this linkage of worship to spiritual growth in his book *Worship His Majesty*. Specifically examining New Testament worship, Hayford observes:

It is extremely significant that the Apostle Paul twice issued explicit directives to sing psalms, hymns and spiritual songs. He makes it abundantly clear that the purpose for this is to do more than belt out religious tunes, odes and ditties; in fact, song fuels spiritual growth: "Let the word of Christ dwell in you richly . . . singing" (Colossians 3:16), and "Do not be drunk with wine, in which is dissipation; but be filled with the Spirit . . . singing" (Ephesians 5:18-19).[5]

Hayford believes these admonitions of Paul establish the significance of music in New Testament worship.

Look more carefully at Paul's words to Colossian believers:

Let the word of Christ dwell in you richly as you teach and admonish one another with all wisdom, and as you sing psalms, hymns and spiritual songs with gratitude in your hearts to God (Col. 3:16).

Of this passage Hayford suggests, "Here, the fruitful implanting of the Word of God is linked to our singing and worshiping. Most of us would think of these as separate operations—the Word as instructional and song as inspirational." Hayford continues, "But instead, human intellect and emotion are integrated *through* song, and effective teaching is said to require worship for its fullest accomplishment."[6]

Emphasizing the practical power of worship to enhance our grasp of God's Word, Hayford concludes, "Worshipful singing expedites a process that quickens our minds to receive the Word and submits our souls to the Holy Spirit's implanting it within us."[7]

David seemed to understand all this, prophetically perhaps, long before Paul would write to Colossian and Ephesian believers linking spiritual growth to worship. To David, the premier pioneer of praise, worship was always primary.

Throughout the psalms we see additional expressions of worship that emphasize how truly primary this discipline was to King David. He not only set aside more than 10 percent of his entire workforce at the Temple for this ministry (more than a tithe!), but he also practiced it himself. Indeed, David did not have just one specific worship time daily but several. One of David's songs declares, "But I call to God, and the LORD saves me. Evening, morning and noon I cry out" (Ps. 55:16-17). He gives further insight into his daily worship in Psalm 119:164, "Seven times a day I praise you for your righteous laws."

THE CHIEF THING!

Another vital observation regarding the primacy of worship at David's Tabernacle is the fact that worship offered there was directed entirely to the Lord. Read again these words regarding the placing of God's Ark in David's small tent:

> So they brought the Ark of God into the special tent David had prepared for it, and they sacrificed burnt offerings and peace offerings *before God.* David appointed the following Levites to lead the people in worship *before the Ark of the LORD* by asking for his blessings and giving thanks and praise to the LORD, the God of Israel. The priests, Benaiah and Jahaziel, played the trumpets regularly *before the Ark of God's covenant* (1 Chron. 16:1,4,6, *NLT*, emphasis added).

Three times in this brief passage we find the expressions "before God" or "before the Ark." The Ark, of course, represented the very presence of God Himself. The lesson here is that worship was not only open at David's tent, but it was also entirely directed to the Lord. Worship was unto Him, not unto the people.

Too often contemporary worship appears to be directed toward meeting our needs, lifting our spirits, soothing our souls—not that this is always a bad thing. But Davidic worship focused entirely on God. And amazingly, in that atmosphere people's needs were met, spirits were lifted and souls were soothed. God's presence alone can do all that!

Commenting on the fact that David's worship was entirely unto the Lord, Tommy Tenney relates, "David did more than surround the ark of God with sanctified worshipers. He made sure that their primary focus was to minister to God through praise, worship and adoration. The Levites, the Old Testament ministers of worship and praise, stood between the world on the outside and the unveiled glory of God on the inside."[8]

To David, everything pointed to God. Worship was, indeed, primary. Centuries later we would see something of this spirit in Francis of Assisi, who saw in almost everything an occasion for worship. To him worship also was primary. One biographer said of Francis:

Francis saw a tiny worm lying in his path, and he stooped to pick it up, because it was a creature of the Almighty. He saw wildflowers of the fields, but even more he saw the hand of God that made them. He beheld the moon and the stars in the heavens at night, and the sun at midday, and he beheld the love of God reaching down along their beams to embrace the children he had created. Even in suffering, to use the phrase Francis Thompson used many years later, St. Francis saw "the shade of God's hand outstretched caressingly." But always [Francis of] Assisi saw, more than anything else, that all things were intended to touch the heart of men and lift them to God.[9]

This easily could describe David who, nearly two millennia before, desired in every way to lift men's hearts to God. And what David desired then is happening now, dramatically. And it is spreading. The restoration is under way.

Throughout these pages I have suggested that a full restoring of all that we have seen related to David's ancient Tabernacle will sweep across the world in the last days, leading to history's greatest harvest (see Amos 9:11-15; Acts 15:16-18). If such is the case, we can expect intercessory worship to become the main thing in all we do as followers of Christ. True, it may not be the only thing, but it will be the chief thing.

We must evangelize the lost. But we will do it in an atmosphere of intercessory worship. We need to disciple new believers. But worship will be central. We must plant reproducing churches. But worship will be the foundation. We must dig wells, build clinics and feed the hungry. But worship will saturate each task at every step.

We may do many things, but we will keep the main thing the main thing. As in David's day, worship will be primary.

PATHWAY TEN:

STRATEGIC WORSHIP

OPENING HEAVEN'S GATES

"It is no coincidence," Jack Hayford writes, "that Israel's greatest development in worship coincided with her broadest boundaries of government. David was the leader for both."[1] Hayford concludes, "There is no more insightful study in worship than the life and music of David. In worship he soars; with worship he wars."[2]

To David, worship was strategic. It was primary in that worship was the main thing; worship was central to all they did. But worship was primary also because it was strategic.

In the simplest sense, "strategic" refers to that which counts the most. A hill taken in battle is said to be strategic if capturing that hill is critical to winning the battle. To David, worship was critical to winning their battles and, indeed, the entire war.

SUPERNATURAL AMMUNITION

A consultant to our ministry once posed an interesting question to emphasize our need to think strategically. He asked, "If a lone soldier in a battle sees 1,000 enemy soldiers advancing toward him, each with a weapon in hand, and if that soldier has only two cartridges left in his rifle, what's the most strategic use of those two bullets?"

None of our executive team had an answer, convinced that in a real-life situation the poor soldier was doomed.

The consultant responded, "He would look immediately for two specific enemies. First, he'd try to find the one soldier of the thousand who was wearing a sidearm and not carrying a rifle. He would take him out with the first of his two bullets."

The consultant explained, "He would do this because the only soldier with a sidearm would be the commander. To remove the commander would immediately create a vacuum in leadership and cause disarray among the troops."

This made sense, but we all wondered who would be the target of the remaining bullet.

The consultant continued, "Then, the lone soldier would look for the man without a weapon but carrying a walkie-talkie. With his second bullet he would take him out."

Noting our confused looks, the consultant concluded, "The lone soldier would shoot the man with the walkie-talkie because he is in charge of communication. If this person were no longer able to communicate with their support force or base, more confusion would result. The remaining troops might find themselves in even greater disarray and possibly be forced to retreat for lack of both leadership and communication."

To David, worship before God provided supernatural ammunition against the enemy. He thought strategically. David had one bullet—worship—and it was all he needed. Hayford is right about David's worship strategy: "In worship he soars; with worship he wars."

Throughout the Davidic psalms, we discover, rather frequently, how spiritual warfare is uniquely woven together with themes of worship. One of David's psalms that begins with the words, "I love you, O LORD, my strength. I call to the LORD, who is worthy of praise" (Ps. 18:1,3), quickly transitions to a warfare theme declaring:

> It is God who arms me with strength and makes my way perfect. He makes my feet like the feet of a deer; he enables me to stand on the heights. He trains my hands for battle; my arms can bend a bow of bronze. You give me your shield of victory and your right hand sustains me; you stoop down to make me great. You broaden the path beneath me, so that my ankles do not turn (vv. 32-36).

Elsewhere in Psalms we discover a similar theme. David sang, "Praise be to the LORD my rock, who trains my hands for war, my fingers for battle" (Ps. 144:1). In an earlier psalm we read, "But you have raised a banner for those who honor you—a rallying point in the face of attack" (Ps. 60:4, *NLT*).

Especially familiar is this declaration of praise: "May God arise, may his enemies be scattered; may his foes flee before him" (Ps. 68:1). This is a reference back to God's glory cloud rising during Israel's journeys in the wilderness and how the cloud served as a symbol of God's presence as He went before His people into battle.

A HARVEST SONG

In all of these Davidic psalms we see a clear relationship between strategic warfare and strategic worship. It is a scene that many prayer practitioners of our day understand. I have met few prayer leaders who have traveled to distant places throughout the world for prayer initiatives who did not understand the strategic significance of intercessory worship. Most would never move into a sustained time of focused intercession without considerable time devoted to worship. They understand its strategic importance.

Joseph Garlington is one such leader. Of the strategic power of worship Garlington wrote, "If the music of David deployed on a single instrument literally drove evil spirits away from King Saul (1 Samuel 16:23), then we need to wage Spirit-led warfare by worshiping God and playing on a hundred or a thousand instruments."[3]

Further linking worship with warfare, Garlington suggests, "Anything God accomplishes in the earth is done through spiritual means using spiritual people. The giving of tithes, offerings, and the gifts of the Spirit are acts of war. Praising God is an act of war. Worshiping God is an act of war. Prayer is an act of war. Fasting is an act of war."[4]

> We are indeed at war, and intercessory worship may well become our most strategic weapon.

We are indeed at war, and intercessory worship may well become our most strategic weapon. At stake in this war are multitudes of future believers from every tribe, tongue, people and nation, who will someday worship God before His throne (see Rev. 7:9-10).

If "strategic" refers to that which counts the most, surely the souls of these vast multitudes fall into that category. Entire nations and people groups ultimately being redeemed are at stake in this war.

Interestingly, we see this very focus and theme permeating the worship of David when he sets up his tent on that modest mountain (which was more of a mound) that we call Mount Zion. It is amazing that at that celebration (see

1 Chron. 16) David sang of the Great Commission 1,000 years before Christ spoke it! David's was a harvest song.

Look again at the events surrounding the placing of the Ark in that small tent when David moved it from Gibeon to Jerusalem. When the Ark was finally placed in the tent, David sang a song that in our various present translations embodies but 30 verses of Scripture. It is remarkable in this relatively brief song how often David links their worship to impacting the entire world. Consider these Scriptures:

That day David gave to Asaph and his fellow Levites this song of thanksgiving to the LORD: Give thanks to the LORD and proclaim his greatness. *Let the world know* what he has done. Sing to him; yes, sing his praises. *Tell everyone* about his miracles. *Let the whole earth sing* to the LORD! Each day *proclaim the good news* that he saves. *Publish his glorious deeds among the nations. Tell everyone* about the amazing things he does. *O nations of the world, recognize the LORD,* recognize that the LORD is glorious and strong. *Let all the earth tremble* before him. *The world is firmly established* and cannot be shaken. Let the heavens be glad, and *let the earth rejoice! Tell all the nations* that the LORD is King (1 Chron. 16:7-9,23-24,28,30-31, *NLT*; emphasis added).

It is amazing that in this single, relatively brief song of David, there are at least 10 references to the nations, peoples, world or Earth being impacted as the result of their worship. Note the phrases "let the world know"; "tell everyone"; "let the whole earth sing"; "proclaim the good news"; "publish his glorious deeds among the nations"; "O nations . . . recognize the LORD"; "let all the earth tremble"; "the world is firmly established, let the earth rejoice"; and "tell all the nations that the LORD is King!" Can there be any question that David possessed a worshiper's world vision?

THE GREAT CONNECTION

It cannot be a mere coincidence that when David set up his tent for the Ark of God's presence, his song strategically focused on all the world. And there can be no mistaking the connection to the ultimate last-days restoration of the Tabernacle of David and God's ultimate harvest. Along with the Great Commission, we must recognize the "Great Connection"—that of intercessory worship and the end-time harvest.

David was a man after God's own heart, and the heart of God clearly encompasses all the world. I believe David's song at the Tabernacle dedication was not just his own song, but a song the Holy Spirit was also singing through him. It is a song I am certain God wants to sing through us in a thousand different ways, calling in His harvest.

The strategic tie of worship to the harvest is something John Piper addresses powerfully and beautifully in his book *Let the Nations Be Glad.* Piper especially helped me see the ministry I lead, Every Home for Christ, in a fresh light. I have always thought of EHC as a ministry primarily seeking to win souls through home-to-home evangelism by systematically planting seeds of the gospel message. And the Lord has been gracious to grant encouraging fruit.

Over EHC's 55-year history, God has allowed the planting of over 2 billion printed salvation messages in 190 countries. More than 27 million decision cards have been returned and followed up on by Christian workers.

But Piper helped me see that we were doing much more than just bringing souls into the Kingdom—not that this is in any way insignificant. Additionally, wonderfully, we are helping mobilize redeemed worshipers by the millions, who are being added to that awesome multitude of eternal worshipers that no one could count (see Rev. 7:9). What a glorious assignment!

John Piper also helped me see the Great Commission in a new light—the light of worship. This insight from Piper was especially helpful:

> God is pursuing with omnipotent passion a world-wide purpose of gathering joyful worshippers for himself from every tribe and tongue and people and nation. Therefore let us bring our affections into line with his, and, for the sake of his name, let us renounce the quest for worldly comforts, and join his global purpose. If we do this, God's omnipotent commitment to his name will be over us like a banner, and we will not lose, in spite of many tribulations (Acts 9:16; Romans 8:35-39). Missions is not the ultimate goal of the church. Worship is. Missions exists because worship doesn't. The Great Commission is first to delight yourself in the Lord (Psalm 37:4). And then to declare, "Let the nations be glad and sing for joy!" (Psalm 67:4).[5]

GOD'S PLAN

Because I believe God has called me, at least to some degree, into that category of those who might be labeled as mission strategists, I pondered the practicality of intercessory worship and David's Tabernacle being restored as it related to simply fulfilling a particular ministry mandate, any mandate. At Every Home for Christ, our mandate is to help fulfill the Great Commission by seeing a presentation of the gospel taken to every home in the entire world. So to respond to our mandate, we prayerfully decided to develop a 10-year plan to move us toward this objective.

As our global leadership team took a strategic look at this ambitious goal to see what it would take to accomplish the task, we were repeatedly challenged by what seemed to be insurmountable obstacles. Consider, for example, more than 100 million Muslim homes in the Middle East, where restrictions seemingly stop us dead in our tracks. This could be cause to give up, were it not for similar circumstances in Soviet Russia just a decade or so ago that changed almost overnight. EHC has now visited over 40 million homes in Russia and the rest of the former Soviet Union.

Besides government restrictions, there were other huge obstacles as well. The cost of fulfilling our total mandate was daunting—at least a quarter-billion dollars. We knew we could not do it alone, and we also realized that, although the Body of Christ already might easily have the resources to do it, much of what is presently being done is seriously uncoordinated, often unnecessarily duplicated and frequently downright sectarian.

We have actually seen evangelical Christian ministries and denominations, for example, that have spent considerable sums of money producing literature and books, not to evangelize the lost, but to refute the teachings of others who are trying to evangelize the lost. Thus, the first message some nonbelievers ever receive related to the gospel is not a message of hope in Christ but a message telling them why someone else's teaching is false. Imagine that!

So it seemed that we had our work cut out for us. Still, we were driven by a realization that God's overall plan will ultimately be accomplished. And we further believed God was leading us to draft a 10-year plan that fit into His overall plan. We knew we could not do it all, but we also realized we could do our part. Further, if all the critical parts came together in Christ, then through all we could do it all!

In the midst of drafting our 10-year plan, on one particular day when we faced some especially difficult challenges, I was encouraged by a promise from Isaiah that fell into that day's Bible-reading assignment. I read:

I have a plan for the whole earth, for my mighty power reaches throughout the world. The LORD Almighty has spoken—who can change his plans? When his hand moves, who can stop him? (Isa. 14:26-27, *NLT*).

God, indeed, has a plan, and it is a plan for the whole earth. We just had to tap into it.

As our team worshiped, worked and prayed together, seeking God for our specific part in His global plan, three clear thoughts came to my mind: (1) a strategic definition, (2) a strategic opportunity and (3) a strategic component.[6]

It quickly became obvious that the restoration of David's Tabernacle was central to God's plan, but we realized that we certainly could not restore that by ourselves. Still, I wondered, could intercessory worship make all this work?

A STRATEGIC DEFINITION

I knew we had to begin by getting a handle on a couple questions: Why did we feel our work was strategic? How does intercessory worship fit in?

Was not our specific objective just a small part of many other good things being done in Christ's Body? And what do we really mean when we speak about fulfilling the Great Commission? Further, would the Body of Christ ever truly come together to see this mandate measurably fulfilled? Some observations, and a few answers, began to come.

Although there are a variety of ways we might define what the Church refers to as the Great Commission, most agree that the supreme mandate Christ gave the Church is to provide a clear presentation of His good news to every person on Earth (see Mark 16:15) and then disciple those who respond (see Matt. 28:19) so that they might, in turn, witness to and disciple still others until the whole world is evangelized. We know world evangelism is God's will—He desires everyone to be saved (see 2 Pet. 3:9; 1 Tim. 2:1-4). When this is defined in the context of a military-style campaign, with the objective of total victory, three clarifications come to mind.

1. The Tactical Approach to Evangelism and Discipleship

"Tactics" is defined as "the science of arranging and maneuvering forces in action against an enemy."[7] "Tactics" is also defined as "any method used to gain an end" or "skillful methods or procedures."[8] Most of the hundreds of evangelism and discipleship plans today are tactical in their approach and in a military context, and tend to lead to a methodology that, although unintentional, might be defined as guerrilla in nature.

2. The Guerrilla Approach to Evangelism and Discipleship

Andy Duda, our Every Home for Christ board chairman, started me thinking on all this while sketching some thoughts on a white board during our strategic planning process. Describing in general the various tactics of a multitude of Christian efforts and noting how little progress Christ's Body seems to be making at times in substantially finishing the task of fulfilling the Great Commission, Andy said, "Sometimes I think the Church is like many disjointed guerrilla forces, all disconnected, who come out of hiding in the hills from time to time just to irritate the enemy. Then they all run back into the hills to hide. These forces never seem to get together long enough to finish off the enemy."

Andy hit the nail on the head and hammered home some key insights to shape my thinking on guerrilla evangelism versus strategic evangelism.

Generally speaking, guerrilla warfare tends to be more disruptive in nature than truly strategic. True, in some cases persistent guerrilla warfare—harassing the enemy whenever and wherever possible—can produce strategic results and lead to ultimate victory. However, most often guerrilla warfare results in merely irritating an enemy until some clear-cut, sweeping strategy falls into place, leading to the total defeat of that enemy.

Much of evangelism and church planting in the world today appears to be of a guerrilla nature, consisting of a multitude of often-disjointed campaigns that tend to harass the enemy rather than seize all of his territory and bring about his total defeat. It is time we think strategically, which I believe will happen as David's Tabernacle is truly restored.

3. The Strategic Approach to Evangelism and Discipleship

Webster defines "strategic" as "that which is essential to victory" or "a plan of action that is required to achieve a stated goal."[9] Strategic evangelism, then, can only be truly strategic if it has a measurable way to provide everyone everywhere with the gospel.

Further, strategic discipleship must, according to this definition, include a plan to meaningfully and measurably disciple everyone, not just a high percentage, of all those who respond to the gospel. This is actually more plausible than one may imagine—if many more Christian entities unite together.

Thus, any truly strategic plan must ultimately attempt to link together as many of the tactical and guerrilla evangelism and discipleship entities as possible, in such a sweeping way that, by its very nature, the total plan becomes essential for victory. The victory is, of course, the literal completion of the Great Commission.

It soon became clear that God was placing before us a wonderful opportunity to be a part of an emerging strategy toward this goal.

A STRATEGIC OPPORTUNITY

Dr. Todd Johnson, missions researcher and coauthor with Dr. David Barrett of the newly updated *World Christian Encyclopedia*, evaluated the progress of global missions in light of the new millennium at a consultation in Colorado Springs in March 1999. According to Dr. Johnson, there have been more than 1,500 global plans among both denominational and parachurch organizations in the past two decades. Each of these plans focused on some aspect of completing the Great Commission by the year 2000.

Sadly, as Johnson explained, the vast majority of these plans, though voicing a commitment to cooperation and partnership, have pretty much functioned independently. True, many have gathered for large consultations to report on their activities, but when those consultations concluded, only modest strategic partnering had occurred. Thankfully, some, such as Phil Butler of the ministry called Interdev, have kept the partnering spirit alive, though I believe God has plans for much, much more in the days ahead.[10]

Dr. Johnson then shared several factors that he believed were essential to measurably seeing the completion of the Great Commission. Included in the list were such obvious factors as less duplication of ministry effort, increased strategic cooperation and planning, and similar ideas.

Presenting statistical data to back up his claims, Johnson pointed out that unless God opens up a way to truly unite these independent plans in a far more focused manner, by the year 2020 there will still be 6,000 unreached people groups by any of today's standard definitions of least-evangelized groups. The unreached groups will be even larger than today, with even greater numbers yet to be evangelized.[11]

Although this was understandably a negative assessment, I found my heart rejoicing in how God had been leading Every Home for Christ to establish The Jericho Center. I felt God would use it to help, if only modestly, reverse these trends.

The center, we had determined, would be committed to hosting regular consultations of various potential participating entities that were willing to be a part of strategic alliances for evangelism and discipleship. The consultations would relate to a fourfold process that we viewed as links toward completing the Great Commission. They included: planning, equipping, going and discipling.

1. The Planning Link

The planning link would include everything from gathering critical research data for potentially united evangelism and discipleship projects, to organizing prayer teams and intercessory worship networks to saturate these projects in prayer. The already-existing World Prayer Center in Colorado Springs would be a vital part of this aspect.[12]

Also a part of this first link would be seeking ways to resource all the various elements or ministries needed to complete a project. For example, business leaders' consultations would be held to see the release of resources, not just for one ministry, but for many, as they worked together toward the same goal.

2. The Equipping Link

The equipping link would involve ministries, agencies and denominations that specialize in training or equipping for the tasks of evangelism, discipleship and church planting. This link would also include those who provide tools to help in the process of spreading the gospel.

For example, literature and Bible publishers are equippers. Producers of tools like the *Jesus* film fall into this category. Consultations would be held targeting specific regions or nations, seeking ways to unite these ministry resources much more effectively for the completion of the Great Commission.

3. The Going Link

The going link represents ministries, agencies or groups focusing on both mass and personal evangelism (i.e., anyone who goes with the gospel). This, of course, includes a vast array of possibilities since almost all ministries somehow view their mandate as contributing to this category.

Imagine even a modest number of these groups beginning to come together in practical alliances to allow their tactical efforts to overlap into one sweeping strategy.

Target, for example, a nation like Tibet for 18 months with both humanitarian "goers" and evangelism "goers" working in tandem, and that nation could begin to see the seeds planted for a true spiritual transformation.

4. The Discipleship Link

The discipleship link, of course, represents the end result in the entire process. All of our evangelism efforts are clearly ineffective unless they reproduce maturing followers of Jesus.

Thus, something must happen to bring together groups and ministry strategies that concentrate on discipling new believers. There are scores of such agencies, in addition to many significant evangelical denominational programs committed to discipleship.

Again, picture a modest number of these groups sitting down and plotting and planning a sweeping strategy to disciple new believers.

This is not to suggest that little has previously happened in this regard (the DAWN strategy, Discipling A Whole Nation, is one encouraging example), but much, much more could happen (even in cooperation with the DAWN model).[13]

Imagine consultations conducted on a regular basis that focused specifically on each of these four links as they touch one particular geographic region or nation, seeking to align these various participating entities into a cohesive, strategic Great Commission force!

In discussing what it would take for this to happen, it became clear that most consultations, at the outset, would need to be intentionally moderate in size, seeking to bring together true decision-makers who, after leaving the planning sessions, could be directly involved in implementing their particular contribution to the overall objectives of a particular project. They would do this in direct cooperation with other strategic partners involved in the same project.

But is any of this realistic in light of the way many ministries, denominations and missions agencies tend to do business? True, there is some measure of isolated partnering, but could something like this happen on a sweeping scale? If so, how? To me, the destinies of many nations depends on it. I believe one key component could make the difference. And it is the subject of this entire book: intercessory worship.

A STRATEGIC COMPONENT

I believe intercessory worship is that key component. For

this reason, a foundational goal of The Jericho Center is to sustain a 24-hour covering of worship and intercessory prayer for the strategic consultations to be hosted at the center, as well as the plans that will result. It is not known if such a strategic component of on-site intercessory worship has ever been directly linked to an ongoing consultation process that seeks to develop such sweeping strategic alliances for evangelism, discipleship and church planting.

Central to this desire for continuous praise and intercession is that biblical picture of Revelation 5:8-10, highlighted in chapter 1. Revelation 5:8 tells of the glorious living creatures and the 24 elders each holding in one hand a harp (symbolic of worship) and in the other hand a golden bowl full of incense, which is the prayers of the saints (symbolic of intercession).

As stated earlier, the linking of these symbols to the ingathering of the harvest is immediately followed in the text by the corporate pronouncement directed to the Lamb of God Himself in the form of a new song, "You are worthy to take the scroll and to open its seals, because you were slain, and with your blood you purchased men for God from every tribe and language and people and nation" (v. 9).

Just how essential is worship combined with intercession to completing the Great Commission? Meditate again on these words of John Piper: "Missions exists today because worship doesn't. Missions is a temporary necessity but worship goes on forever. Therefore, worship is both the fuel and the goal of missions."[14]

Return with me again to the overall theme of this book: pathways for the restoration of the Tabernacle of David. You will remember that the apostle James is defending the evangelization of the Gentiles at the Council of Jerusalem (see Acts 15:15-18) when he quotes a rather obscure prophecy from Amos 9:11-12, as we explained in chapter 1. Let's look at it again as we build a case for its strategic connection to a vast end-time harvest:

> In that day I will restore the fallen kingdom of David. It is now like a house in ruins, but I will rebuild its walls and restore its former glory. And Israel will possess what is left of Edom and all the nations I have called to be mine. I, the LORD, have spoken, and I will do these things (Amos 9:11-12, *NLT*).

Note again that the reference in Amos 9 to possessing

the remnant of Edom was terminology used in Amos's day to mean possessing the Gentiles. This is why James relates that David's Tabernacle will be restored so that "the rest of mankind may seek the LORD, even all the Gentiles" (Acts 15:17, *NKJV*). Mike Bickle says of the Amos 9 passage and James's reference to it:

> James was recalling God's promise to restore the Tabernacle of David—which is the very embodiment of intercessory worship before the beauty, holiness, and glory of God—as a means of releasing the fullness of salvation and revival for all the nations. This model of intercessory worship will be restored so that the Great Commission can be completed—so that every tribe, tongue and nation will be present on the last day (Revelation 5:9, 7:9-10, 14:6, 15:4; Matthew 24:14).[15]

HEAVEN'S GATES

I fully agree with Mike Bickle's connection of intercessory worship to the fulfilling of the Great Commission. Bickle further asks:

What does the restoration of the Tabernacle of David mean to the Church today? I believe it means much more than incorporating the priestly worship and prayer practiced before the Davidic tabernacle. I believe it points the way for us to become a united, victorious apostolic Church that walks in mature love and reaches and reaps the great harvest in all the nations.[16]

Kevin Conner, whose in-depth study on the Tabernacle of David helped me immeasurably in developing these insights, also concurs. In his book *The Tabernacle of David*, Conner offers this concluding observation:

Our study is complete. Under the outpouring of the Holy Spirit in the early church on both the Jew and Gentile, James, by a word of wisdom quoted the prophecy of Amos concerning the building of the Tabernacle of David. The whole purpose of this was for the coming in of the Gentiles. The Gentiles were not to be placed under the law, that is, in the Tabernacle of Moses under the Old Covenant. They were to come in on the ground of grace, that is, into the

Tabernacle of David, which was symbolic of the New Covenant. In this tabernacle, a Jew and Gentile would become one in Christ on the ground of grace, apart from the works of the Law and ceremonials of the Law Covenant.[17]

Think of all this happening in our very lifetime. Could it be that some of what I have suggested in this final chapter is truly possible?

Remember those consultations I spoke of earlier? One wonders what might happen if all these strategic consultations and their resulting alliances were bathed in both continuous worship (inviting God's supreme presence) as well as continuous intercession (entreating God's supernatural power) to truly see the Great Commission completed.

Further imagine that each God-saturated consultation would have one primary objective: God's agenda for each organization or ministry as we corporately link together into one entity to honor Christ everywhere.

Can you picture ministries and agencies of all sorts laying their egos and ambitions before the Lord to see His purposes fulfilled as His children truly unite?

I believe that one of the primary keys to this happening is intercessory worship. Will we recognize it and use it?

Tommy Tenney offers this optimism:

> The thing God promised is going to happen, and a flood of God's glory is going to come. It is going to start somewhere with someone, but where? Who will find the ancient keys that jingled in the hands of God when He told Peter, "Here are the keys to the kingdom. Whatever you open on earth will be opened in Heaven"? Who will hear a knock at the other side and slip that ancient key into that door to open the gate of Heaven? Wherever it happens, whoever opens that door, the result will be an unstoppable, immeasurable flood of the glory of God. If the glory of God is going to cover the earth, it has to start somewhere. Why not here? Why not you?[18]

Could what we have been suggesting on these final pages be just such a key? Is Christ's Body ready to open heaven's gates and release a global baptism of God's glory through an intercessory worship movement that restores the Tabernacle of David so "the rest of humanity might find the Lord"? (Acts 15:17, *NLT*).

This is, indeed, an exciting time to be alive. It is a time to set our sights on finishing the task of world evangelization. It is a time to transform our families, cities and nations. But let's not miss our ultimate goal in the process. John Piper keeps it before us when he writes:

> All of history is moving toward one great goal, the white-hot worship of God and His Son among all the peoples of the earth. Missions is not that goal. It is the means. And for that reason it is the second greatest human activity in the world.[19]

Let's not forget the first—and we will surely succeed at the second!

ENDNOTES

Chapter One

1. The name has been changed because the worshiper wished to remain anonymous.
2. Joseph Garlington, *Worship: The Pattern of Things in Heaven* (Shippensburg, PA: Destiny Image Publishers, Inc., 1997), p. 1, quoted in *Heights of Delight* (Ventura, CA: Regal Books, 2002), p. 41.

Chapter Two

1. Kevin J. Conner, *The Tabernacle of David* (Portland, OR: CIM Bible Publishing, KJC Publications, 1976), p. 79.
2. Ibid., p. 80.
3. Philip Yancey, *Reaching for the Invisible God* (Grand Rapids, MI: Zondervan Publishing House, 2000), p. 192.

4. James Strong, *The Exhaustive Concordance of the Bible*, "A Concise Dictionary of the Words in the Hebrew Bible" (Nashville, TN: Abingdon, 1894), s.v. "sookah."

5. Ibid., s.v. "skene."

6. Mike Bickle, "The Tabernacle of David," *Pray!* vol. 19 (July/August 2000), p. 19.

7. Conner, *The Tabernacle of David*, p. 11.

8. Ibid., p. 12.

9. Ibid., p. 17.

10. Ibid.

11. Tommy Tenney, *God's Favorite House* (Shippensburg, PA: Destiny Image Publishers, Inc., 1999), p. 5.

12. Conner, *The Tabernacle of David*, p. 28.

13. Ibid.

14. Ibid.

15. Ibid.

16. Ibid., p. 81.

17. Ibid.

18. Robert Stearns, *The Tabernacle of David*, audiotapes of lectures (Clarence, NY: Kairos Publications, n.d.).

19. Ibid.

20. Dr. Edward W. Li, *Science and Faith* (Singapore: Every Home Crusade Co., Ltd.). For more information regarding this book, contact Every Home for Christ at Singapore: Every Home Crusade Co., Ltd., No. 8, Lorong 27-A, Geylong Road #02-04, Gulin Building 388106 or by e-mail at elicspore@singnet.com.sg.

21. Ibid., p. 24.

22. Ibid., p. 25.

Chapter Three

1. Tommy Tenney, *God's Favorite House* (Shippensburg, PA: Destiny Image Publishers, Inc., 1999), p. 9.

2. *Vine's Expository Dictionary of Old Testament Words* (Bible Explorer Epiphany Software, San Jose: CA, 1999), s.v. "tamiyd."

3. A. W. Tozer, *Whatever Happened to Worship?* (Camp Hill, PA: Christian Publications, 1985), p. 24.

4. Ibid.

5. Tenney, *God's Favorite House*, pp. 51-52.

6. Ibid., p. 142.

7. Ibid., p. 141.

8. Joseph Garlington, *Worship: The Pattern of Things in Heaven* (Shippensburg, PA: Destiny Image Publishers, Inc., 1997), p. 58.

9. Leslie K. Tarr, "The Prayer Meeting that Lasted 100 Years," *Decision Magazine* (May 1977), p. 14.

10. Ibid.

11. Ibid.

12. Ibid.

Chapter Four

1. Aristotle, *Nicomachean Ethics*, circa 350 B.C.

2. James Strong, *The Exhaustive Concordance of the Bible*, "A Concise Dictionary of the Words in the Hebrew Bible" (Nashville, TN: Abingdon, 1894), s.v. "kabod."

3. Ibid., s.v. "hadar."

4. Ibid., s.v. "howd."

5. *Webster's New World Dictionary*, 3rd ed., s.v. "unique."

6. Ibid., s.v. "diversity."

7. Audrey Mieir, *His Name Is Wonderful*, copyright 1959, renewed 1987 by Manna Music, Inc. All rights reserved. Used by permission.

8. Paul Balouche, *Open the Eyes of My Heart*, 1997, Integrity's Hosanna! Music/ASCAP.

9. Mike Bickle (message spoken at New Life Church, Colorado Springs, CO, April 9, 1999).

Chapter Five

1. Evangeline Booth, quoted in Kevin J. Conner, *The Tabernacle of David* (Portland, OR: CIM Bible Publishing, KJC Publications, 1976), p. 181.

2. Jack W. Hayford, *Worship His Majesty* (Waco, TX: Word Books, 1987), p. 163.

3. Joseph Garlington, *Worship: The Pattern of Things in Heaven* (Shippensburg, PA: Destiny Image Publishers, Inc., 1997), p. 140.

4. Ibid., p. 152.

5. Ibid., p. 143.

6. Sharon Begley, "Music on the Mind," *Newsweek* (July 24, 2000), p. 50.

7. Ibid., p. 51.

8. Ibid.

9. Ibid.

10. Brother Lawrence, *The Practice of the Presence of God* (Old Tappan, NJ: Spire Books, Fleming H. Revell Co., 1958), p. 45.

11. Garlington, *Worship*, p. 144.

Chapter Six

1. Saint Augustine, *Patrologia Latina,* quoted in Dick Eastman, *A Celebration of Praise* (Grand Rapids, MI: Baker Book House, 1984), p. 9.

2. Jack W. Hayford, *Worship His Majesty* (Waco, TX: Word Books, 1987), p. 134.

3. Ibid.

4. A. W. Tozer, *Whatever Happened to Worship* (Camp Hill, PA: Christian Publications, 1985), p. 43.

5. Mike Bickle, "The Tabernacle of David," *Pray!* vol. 19 (July/August 2000), p. 19.

6. Ibid., p. 18.

7. Jerry Savelle, "The Force of Joy" (presented at a plenary session of the Maranatha Ministries Congress, Ft. Worth, TX, December 1982).

8. Russell Shubin, "Worship That Moves the Soul: A Conversation with Roberta King," *Frontiers* (June 2001), p. 13.

9. Ibid.

10. Ibid.

11. Since Every Home for Christ's beginning in 1946 in Western Canada, 2.02 billion printed gospel messages (with decision cards) have been planted home by home throughout the world. Because two booklets, one for adults and one for children, are often given out at each home, this means at least 1 billion homes have now been reached. Based on the estimated number of people who live in each home and the fact that some homes in the above number were reached more than once (in nations

with multiple coverages, like India), it is estimated that 750 million to 1 billion homes are yet to be reached, with approximately 335 million of these homes in China.

Chapter Seven

1. *American Heritage Dictionary of the English Language*, 4th ed., s.v. "extravagant."

2. Tommy Tenney, *God's Favorite House* (Shippensburg, PA: Destiny Image Publishers, Inc., 1999), p. 34.

3. Tommy Tenney suggests this. He writes: "When David made his second attempt to bring the Ark to Jerusalem, he carefully followed God's instructions. In fact, every six paces they would sacrifice an ox." Tommy Tenney, *God's Favorite House* (Shippensburg, PA: Destiny Image Publishers, Inc., 1999), p. 34.

4. Ron Campbell (statement at a strategic prayer summit in Washington, DC, July 2, 2001, regarding his findings on Freemasonry as outlined in his book *Free from Free Masonry* [Ventura, CA: Regal Books, 1999]).

Chapter Eight

1. Dick Eastman, *The Jericho Hour* (Orlando, FL: Creation House, 1994), pp. 166-173.

2. Ibid., p. 169.

3. John Piper, *Let the Nations Be Glad* (Grand Rapids, MI: Baker Book House, 1993), p. 12.

4. Madame Guyon, *Autobiography* (Chicago, IL: Moody Press, 1980), p. 16.

Chapter Nine

1. A. W. Tozer, *Whatever Happened to Worship* (Camp Hill, PA: Christian Publications, 1985), p. 14.

2. Jack W. Hayford, *Worship His Majesty* (Waco, TX: Word Books, 1987), p. 148.

3. Ibid., p. 149.

4. Joseph Garlington, *Worship: The Pattern of Things in Heaven* (Shippensburg, PA: Destiny Image Publishers, Inc.), p. 26.

5. James Strong, *The Exhaustive Concordance of the Bible*, "A Concise Dictionary of the Words in the Hebrew Bible" (Nashville, TN: Abingdon, 1894), s.v. "machowl."

6. Ibid., s.v. "karar."

7. Ibid., s.v. "raqad."

8. Ibid., s.v. "agalliao."

9. Tozer, *Whatever Happened to Worship*, p. 82.

10. Ibid., p. 84.

11. Tommy Tenney, *God's Favorite House* (Shippensburg, PA: Destiny Image Publishers, Inc., 1999), p. 22.

12. Garlington, *Worship*, p. 27.

Chapter Ten

1. Mike Bickle, "The Tabernacle of David," *Pray!* vol. 19 (July/August 2000), p. 19.

2. Ibid.

3. Joseph Garlington, *Worship: The Pattern of Things in Heaven* (Shippensburg, PA: Destiny Image Publishers, Inc.), p. 130.

4. Ibid.

5. Ibid., p. 132.

6. Tommy Tenney, *God's Favorite House* (Shippensburg, PA: Destiny Image Publishers, Inc., 1999), pp. 8-9.

7. Bickle, "The Tabernacle of David," p. 19.

Chapter Eleven

1. A. W. Tozer, *Whatever Happened to Worship* (Camp Hill, PA: Christian Publications, 1985), p. 56.

2. Ibid.

3. John Piper, *Let the Nations Be Glad* (Grand Rapids, MI: Baker Book House, 1993), p. 14.

4. Ibid., p. 38.

5. Jack W. Hayford, *Worship His Majesty* (Waco, TX: Word Books, 1987), pp. 164-165.

6. Ibid., p. 165.

7. Ibid., p. 166.

8. Tommy Tenney, *God's Favorite House* (Shippensburg, PA: Destiny Image Publishers, Inc., 1999), pp. 57-58.

9. *The Writings of Saint Francis of Assisi*, trans. Benen Fahy (Chicago, IL: Franciscan Herald Press, 1976), p. 127.

Chapter Twelve

1. Jack Hayford, *Worship His Majesty* (Waco, TX: Word Books, 1987), p. 129.

2. Ibid., p. 130.

3. Joseph Garlington, *Worship: The Pattern of Things in Heaven* (Shippensburg, PA: Destiny Image Publishers, Inc.), p. 59.

4. Ibid., p. 79.

5. John Piper, *Let the Nations Be Glad* (Grand Rapids, MI: Baker Book House, 1993) p. 40.

6. For a CD-ROM of a partial presentation of Every Home for Christ's *Complete the Commission* strategy write to Every Home for Christ, P.O. Box 35930, Colorado Springs, CO 80935.

7. *Webster's New World Dictionary,* 3rd ed., s.v. "tactics."

8. Ibid.

9. Ibid., s.v. "strategic."

10. Dr. Todd Johnson (presented at the closing session of The Watchword in World Missions Consultation, Colorado Springs, Co, March 1999).

11. Interdev, a respected ministry headed by Phil Butler, seeks to form strategic partnerships to help fulfill the Great Commission. For information about Interdev, contact them by post at 6912 220th St., S.W., Suite 302, Mountlake Terrace, WA 98043; by phone at 425-775-8330; by fax 425-775-8326; or by e-mail at Interdev-us@xc.org.

12. The World Prayer Center, associated with New Life Church, Colorado Springs, Colorado, seeks to link hundreds of prayer networks and local church prayer gatherings to join together in praying for a worldwide awakening. They help to mobilize a strategic, undergirding prayer for all the projects involving alliances created through The Jericho Center. You may contact the World Prayer Center by post at The World Prayer Center, 11005 Hwy. 83, Colorado Springs, CO, 80920, or by e-mail at info@wpccs.org.

13. DAWN Ministries (Disciple A Whole Nation) was founded by Dr. Jim Montgomery to help establish saturation church-planting initiatives in nations throughout the world. At the time of this publication, 154 nations have full-scale DAWN initiatives. You may contact DAWN by post at DAWN, 5775 N. Union Blvd., Colorado Springs, CO 80918, or by e-mail at dawnbarni@hotmail.com.

14. Piper, *Let the Nations Be Glad*, p. 1.

15. Mike Bickle, "The Tabernacle of David," *Pray!* vol. 19 (July/August 2000) p. 22.

16. Ibid.

17. Kevin J. Conner, *The Tabernacle of David* (Portland, OR: City Bible Publishing, KJC Publications, 1976), p. 253.

18. Tommy Tenney, *God's Favorite House* (Shippensburg, PA: Destiny Image Publishers, 1999), pp. 139-140.

19. Piper, *Let the Nations Be Glad*, p. 15.

Every Home for Christ . . .
Reaching the Nations One Family at a Time!

*E*very Home for Christ, led by Dr. Dick Eastman, author of *Heights of Delight,* is a global home-to-home evangelism ministry (formerly known as World Literature Crusade) that has worked with more than 500 denominations and mission organizations to conduct Every Home Campaigns in 190 nations.

Since its inception, Every Home for Christ, with a full-time staff of over 1,200 workers plus over 2,400 volunteer associates, has distributed over 2.1 billion gospel messages home by home, resulting in over 27.5 million decision cards being mailed to EHC's numerous offices overseas and the establishing of over 43,000 village New Testament fellowships called "Christ Groups." Where illiterate people groups exist, EHC distributes gospel records and audiotapes, including the amazing "card talks" (cardboard record players). In one recent 12-month period 1,485,284 decision cards were received in EHC offices around the world, or an average of 4,069 *every day!*

To date, Every Home Campaigns have been conducted in 190 countries and completed in 90. The EHC ministry presently maintains 100 offices throughout the world, including much of the former Soviet Union and all 32 provinces and autonomous regions of China.

Because some areas of the world are virtually closed to Christian outreach, particularly in Middle Eastern countries, Every Home for Christ has developed an especially strong prayer mobilization effort through its multi-hour *Change the World School of Prayer* originated by Dick Eastman. More than 2,000,000 Christians in 120 nations have been impacted by this training, portions of which are now on DVD (video) in over 50 languages.

EHC's *Feed 5000* campaign enables believers to reach at least 5,000 people with the Gospel, over the course of a year. *Feed 5000* gives individuals a way to put feet to their prayers for the lost by providing gospel booklets and Bible-study materials that present Jesus, "the Bread of Life," for families who need to discover His offer of salvation.

Dick Eastman invites you to learn more about this opportunity by contacting Every Home for Christ for a full-color Lighthouse Edition of EHC's World Prayer Map along with information about how to become involved in feeding 5,000 the Bread of Life annually.

In the USA: Call toll-free 1-800-423-5054
Also, in the USA: 1-719-260-8888
P.O. Box 35930, Colorado Springs, CO 80935
In Canada: 1-800-265-7326
450 Speedvale Ave #101, Guelph, Ontario N1H 7X6
For other global addresses, contact EHC in the USA.
Visit our website at www.ehc.org

Other tools from the author of
"Heights of Delight"...

BEYOND IMAGINATION:
A SIMPLE PLAN TO SAVE
THE WORLD

DICK EASTMAN
ON PRAYER

LIVING AND PRAYING IN
JESUS NAME
CO-AUTHORED WITH JACK HAYFORD

Available from Every Home for Christ—See phone
and address below.

PRACTICAL PRAYER . . .

A FAST-PACED 13-LESSON VIDEO
SERIES BASED ON DICK EASTMAN'S
BEST-SELLING BOOK "THE HOUR
THAT CHANGES THE WORLD."

IDEAL FOR CELL GROUPS, SUNDAY
SCHOOL CLASSES, PRAYER GROUPS,
AND EVEN TEEN-AGE HOME
SCHOOLERS.

In the USA: Call toll-free 1-800-423-5054
Also, in the USA: 1-719-260-8888
P.O. Box 35930, Colorado Springs, CO 80935
In Canada: 1-800-265-7326
450 Speedvale Ave #101, Guelph, Ontario N1H 7X6
For other global addresses, contact EHC in the USA.
Visit our website at www.ehc.org

CHANGE THE WORLD...
From your neighbors to the nations
FREE
from Every Home for Christ

WORLD PRAYER MAP

*A systematic
plan to pray for
every nation on
earth once a
month in just 5
minutes a day!*

*Map includes a place you can sketch
your neighborhood so you can pray daily
for your neighbors.*

Call or write Every Home for Christ to request
your free full-color "lighthouse" edition of EHC's
World Prayer Map. Includes exciting information
on how you can partner with Every Home for
Christ to *Feed 5000* the salvation message in distant
villages throughout the course of a year. (When
writing or calling request *World Prayer Map* and
Feed 5000 information.)

In the USA: Call toll-free 1-800-423-5054
Also, in the USA: 1-719-260-8888
P.O. Box 35930, Colorado Springs, CO 80935
In Canada: 1-800-265-7326
450 Speedvale Ave #101, Guelph, Ontario N1H 7X6
For other global addresses, contact EHC in the USA.
Visit our website at www.ehc.org

Enjoy the Exquisite
Pleasures of God's Eternal Presence

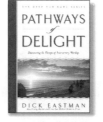

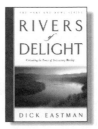

In *Heights of Delight*, the best-selling author of *The Hour That Changes the World* shows how increasing joy in your walk with the Lord is reinforced by the Harp and Bowl—a new approach to prayer in which the harp represents worship and the bowl the incense of prayer.

Pathways of Delight explores worship in all its dimensions—skillful, creative, joyful, extravagant, passionate, open, primary and strategic—and expands upon the basic, overarching subject of intercessory worship while retaining its own distinct message.

Rivers of Delight, the culmination of the trilogy, deals with the prophetic, practical, positional and personal dimensions of worship, citing specific case studies of how praise has opened the heavenlies and led to unique answers to prayer.

Heights of Delight
An Invitation to
Intercessory Worship
Dick Eastman
Gift Hardcover
ISBN 08307.29461

Pathways of Delight
The Restoration of the
Tabernacle of David and
the Destiny of the Nations
Dick Eastman
Gift Hardcover
ISBN 08307.29488

Rivers of Delight
The Flow of Prophetic Worship
and the Healing of Nations
Dick Eastman
Gift Hardcover
ISBN 08307.29496

Available at your local Christian bookstore.
www.regalbooks.com

043738

Regal
God's Word for Your World